Positive
Police
Leadership

Problem-Solving Planning

THOMAS E. BAKER

Looseleaf
Law Publications, Inc.

43-08 162nd Street
Flushing, NY 11358
www.LooseleafLaw.com
800-647-5547

POSITIVE POLICE LEADERSHIP:

PROBLEM-SOLVING PLANNING

Thomas E. Baker

Civilian Police Officer
Special Agent, USACIDC
Lieutenant Colonel, Military Police, USAR
Associate Professor, Criminal Justice

Library of Congress – In Publication Data

Baker, Thomas E., 1941-
    Positive police leadership : problem-solving planning / Thomas E. Baker.
        p. cm.
    Includes bibliographical references and index.
    ISBN 978-1-60885-032-7
1. Police administration--United States. 2. Police--Supervision of--United States. I. Title.
    HV8141.B284 2012
    363.2068'4--dc23

                                                    2011046871

Cover by *Sans Serif,* Saline, Michigan

Cover Photo: New York, NY—Police keep watch as demonstrators associated with the "Occupy Wall Street" movement protest in Times Square on October 15, 2011 in New York City.   *Photo by Mario Tama/Getty Images*

TABLE OF CONTENTS

PART III
POSITIVE POLICE PLANNING AND COACHING

DEDICATION

Positive Police Leadership: Problem-Solving Planning remains dedicated to the men and women of law enforcement, who risk their lives every day to protect our communities and nation. In addition, this book is dedicated to those who serve in the Military Police Corps, and other branches of military service. Those who serve this nation well should always be remembered and honored.

The author would like to recognize Staff Sergeant Jethro Haslett Piland, U.S. Army, who served during World War II, and entered the town of Caen as a member of the D-Day Plus 30 Group. Staff Sergeant Jethro Haslett Piland earned many combat decorations, including the Bronze Star and Silver Star. After the war, Haslett served in the National Guard, and was promoted to the rank of Captain. His brother, Master Sergeant Gordon Alexander Piland, flew 35 missions above war torn Europe, in the 8th Army Air Force. He earned many combat decorations, including the Distinguished Flying Cross.

ACKNOWLEDGMENTS

I would like to thank Jane Piland-Baker, my wife and partner. Her assistance in the area of editorial and graphic illustrations made an immeasurable contribution to the text. A special thank you to the staff at Looseleaf Law Publications, Inc.: Mary Loughrey, Editorial Vice President; Maria Felten, Production Editor; and Michael Loughrey, President.

i

ABOUT THE AUTHOR

Thomas E. Baker is an associate professor of criminal justice at the University of Scranton, and Lt. Col. United States Army Reserve Military Police Corps (Ret.). In addition, Lt. Col. Baker has served as a police officer with Henrico County, Virginia and as an undercover /intelligence officer with the Organized Crime, Vice Intelligence Unit of the Montgomery County Police Department, Maryland.

Lt. Col. Baker's military assignments include: special agent, detachment commander, battalion level commander, and a Command Headquarters assignment with the United States Army Criminal Investigation Command. Additional assignments include: provost marshal, military police investigations, staff officer for Training and Doctrine Command, and instructor for the United States Army Command and General Staff College. He has earned over ten military and national police awards, including the Army Meritorious Service Medal.

Lt. Col. Baker is a graduate of the Basic Military Police Officer's Course, Advanced Infantry Officer's Course, Advanced Military Police Officer's Course, Criminal Investigation Course, Advanced Criminal Investigation Management Course, Psychological Operations Course, Field Grade Infantry Course, and the United States Army Command and General Staff College.

His academic degrees include: A.A. Law Enforcement, B.S. Social Welfare and M.S. Counseling from Virginia Commonwealth University; M.Ed. Sports Science, M.S. Health Education, East Stroudsburg University; CAGS Psychology and Counseling, Marywood College; and Advanced Study Education, Pennsylvania State University and Temple University.

Prof. Baker has been teaching courses at The University of Scranton in criminal justice management, public safety administration, organized crime, criminal investigation, police criminalistics, and criminal analysis for many years.

He is the author of six books and articles in over 170 publications, which have appeared in professional journals, peer-reviewed articles, encyclopedia articles, and has presented research at national meetings. Professor Baker is the author of *Intelligence-Led Policing: Leadership, Strategies, and Tactics*, and *Effective Police Leadership: Moving Beyond Management*, both Looseleaf Law Publications.

PREFACE

A Special Tribute To:

Herman Goldstein made an excellent contribution when he described the Problem-Oriented Policing (POP) process. His work contributed to the proactive policing management era that continues into the future. *Positive Police Leadership: Problem-Solving Planning* seeks to "connect the dots" concerning leadership coordination functions.

Positive Police Leadership: Problem-Solving Planning serves as a primary reader for police officers who aspire to command positions. Police sergeants, lieutenants, and captains will find the leadership applications useful in their efforts to prevent and suppress crime. This text fills the gap concerning police leadership that supports Problem-Oriented Policing (POP) applications.

Positive Police Leadership: Problem-Solving Planning is a Looseleaf Law publication and part of a leadership series of related books. This textbook is directly related to two other Looseleaf Law Publications:

1. *Effective Police Leadership: Moving Beyond Management* (New York: Looseleaf Law Publications, Inc., 3rd Edition, 2010), which focuses on expanded leadership requirements for effective problem-solving.

2. *Intelligence-Led Policing: Leadership, Strategies and Tactics*, (New York: Looseleaf Law Publications, Inc., 2009), which connects the new intelligence management and leadership requirements.

Positive Police Leadership: Problem-Solving Planning is organized and presented in a reader friendly format, which does not require learners to have prerequisite knowledge. The text serves the primary needs of police leaders and officers. However, this text would be useful for community college and university programs. In addition, the text and support materials would be ideally suited to distance education programs.

Target Audience

Readers will find the text interesting because it provides meaningful leadership applications. The text provides systematic and practical applications that support problem-solving skills. Learning progressions enhance the academic destination and construct positive leadership fundamentals.

This book serves as an excellent police resource. Moreover, the book would provide a contribution to national and international libraries, community college, university, and private libraries. The content and foundations serve as a resource text for federal, state, local, and tribal law enforcement agencies.

Educational Philosophy

Positive Police Leadership: Problem-Solving Planning encourages the reader with interesting analytical leadership concepts and solutions to POP leadership problems. The author seeks to avoid dissertation-style writing and attempts to integrate the analytical leadership content and problem-solving process. The case study format and solutions provide simulated learning opportunities.

Structure and Features

Readability, clarity, and theme consistency enhance retention and the learning process. This text strives for clarity in the writing and excellent learning progressions. The paragraphs and sentences are deliberately short and to the point.

The text addresses diverse learning styles; case illustrations and concrete examples clarify concepts and maintain reader interest. Leadership is multifaceted; the text and illustrations enhance reader understanding and retention.

This text emphasizes problem-solving strategies, and tactics. The philosophy and educational approach is dynamic and action-oriented, incorporating critical thinking as a foundation requirement. Critical thinking requires organizing information and applying concepts to new and unique situations.

Instructor-Related Materials

Refer to the related instructor manuals and PowerPoint slides for supporting content for *Positive Police Leadership: Problem-Solving Planning*. For example, *A Test Preparation and Seminar Guide* text package includes supporting PowerPoint and the Problem-Solving Planning and Instructional Testing Guide to assist in implementing the instructional strategies. This text includes case study solutions, goals, objectives, and test-related content. In addition, the PowerPoint presentation supports the instructional content.

This book incorporates an extensive variety of illustrative materials:

- Considerable analytical concepts are presented; therefore, numerous illustrations, models, charts, and tables supplement the text.
- Visual components assist in active explanation of text concepts.
- Subheadings and short paragraphs enhance transition, coherence, and clarity for the learner.
- Large fonts enhance reading under poor lighting conditions, an important consideration for law enforcement officers in the field.

Scope and Organization

Positive Police Leadership: Problem-Solving Planning is divided into Three Parts:

PART I:　POSITIVE PROBLEM-ORIENTED LEADERSHIP
PART II: POSITIVE COMMUNICATION PATHWAYS
PART III: POSITIVE POLICE PLANNING AND COACHING

There are ten basic guideposts and strategies that establish primary policing pathways. The purpose: to establish positive leadership applications, problem-solving strategies, and self-assessment.

Conclusion

Finally, the text emphasizes the need to engage in positive police leadership that results in constructive community outcomes. The pursuit of knowledge concerning police excellence is a worthy goal and that premise serves as the book's foundation. This text deliberately ignores negative illustrations and comments. Everyone knows what poor leadership feels like; the emphasis is on positive leadership attributes.

PART I
POSITIVE POLICE PROBLEM-ORIENTED LEADERSHIP

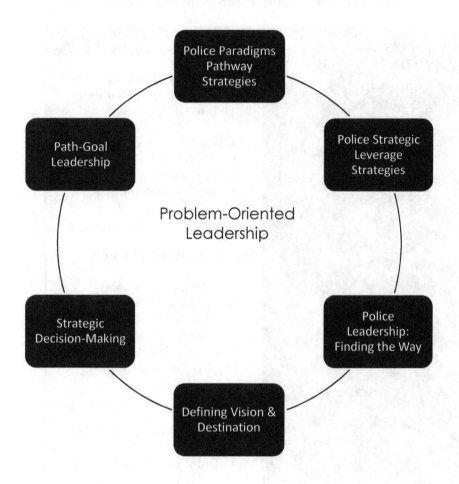

Police Paradigms Pathway Strategies

Police Strategic Leverage Strategies

Path-Goal Leadership

Problem-Oriented Leadership

Police Leadership: Finding the Way

Strategic Decision-Making

Defining Vision & Destination

2

POSITIVE LEADERSHIP FOUNDATIONS GUIDE

Leadership Foundations	Guidepost Behaviors
Police paradigm pathways: • Strategic thinking & influence • Intelligence-led policing • Community-oriented policing • Problem-oriented policing • SARA Planning • CompStat Operations	**Apply 4 steps of Intelligence-Led Policing & Problem-Oriented Policing:** • Apply the Intelligence Cycle • Conduct intelligence analysis • Conduct crime analysis • Apply target analysis
Police leadership applications: • Positive Police Leadership • Emotional Intelligence (EQ) • Leadership pathways • Building teams • Understanding the destination	**Apply 4 leadership steps:** • Path-goal leadership • Align power bases • Team leadership/ participatory management • Win the hearts and minds of police officers and civilians
Police strategic leadership: • Star performance policing • Defining destination • Strategic decision- making • Defining Vision: Destination • Tactical deployment operations	**Apply leadership principles:** • Tell the story and need for change • Define the destination • Teach point of view • Develop storyline. • Examine Tampa Police strategies

CHAPTER 1
POSITIVE POLICE PATHWAYS AND STRATEGIES

"Three changes are especially important to the success of problem-oriented policing: (1) police leaders must articulate the basic values with which they approach the police task and which influence their management techniques; (2) they must have a strong commitment to problem-solving as the core of policing, with all that it entails; and (3) more broadly, they must make fundamental changes in the most common type of relationship that exists between leadership and the rank-and-file in a police agency."

— Herman Goldstein

Change and innovation in policing over the past twenty years are moving at an accelerated rate. Police leaders attempt to keep pace and maintain some balance with shifting organizational, leadership, and technological requirements. Problem-solving solutions require empowering officers and citizens to active participation in the prevention of crime and disorder. The police officer on the beat must establish the leadership and trust necessary for crime prevention.

CHAPTER FOCUS

The twenty-first century requires leaders to be positive, flexible, and adaptable to accelerated change. The text focuses on positive police leadership, emotional intelligence (EQ), and problem-solving skills necessary for influencing change. Quantum leaps into the future require optimistic attentiveness to the human component of problem-solving solutions.

OVERVIEW: POLICE PATHWAYS

The text emphasizes positive leadership and emotional intelligence as the foundation for police problem-solving solutions. Superior police leadership requires confidence, flexibility, and problem-solving skills. Positive solutions demand leadership influence, the application of basic principles, and POP planning.

Positive Police Leadership: Problem- Solving Planning endeavors to build and encourage positive community solutions.

Dedicated police leaders inspire officers into the future and prepare for their contributions to the community and nation. There are many pathways to successful positive police leadership. Ten basic related pathways offer guidance for getting to that future destination. Refer to Figure: 1-1-A for The Ten Basic Leadership Pathways.

Figure 1-1-A: Ten Basic Leadership Pathways

POLICE STAR LEADERSHIP PATHWAYS

Why the need for positive police leadership and problem-solving policing? Insightful police leaders lead from the front; they provide goals and a pathway for officers to follow. Successful police leadership encourages a positive work ethic, productive teamwork, and the problem-solving process. This form of leadership maximizes human potential through corrective insight and emotional intelligence.

Insightful police leadership has the ability to recognize the human dimensions, the necessity for feedback, and its relationship to excellent police performance. Concerned police leaders listen and relate to their officers. This style of leadership is essential when adjusting to rapidly changing community circumstances.

Core Positive Leadership Pathways

- Leadership applications that support a police agency's commitment to maximize officer potential, and encourage proactive policing and community development.
- Leadership that helps officers and their community find effective POP solutions.
- Leadership that inspires service and places the interests of police personnel and community above self-interests.

Positive police leadership demands character strengths and trustworthiness that enhance influence. Problem-solving leadership requirements require high levels of emotional intelligence. Extraordinary police leaders instill inspirational leadership and develop teamwork and collaboration. This kind of leader understands police pathways and chooses them wisely.

Positive Police Leadership Pathways

Why is developing emotional intelligence important? Emotional intelligence is sweeping the nation as the new gold standard for leadership. Many community crime problems can be solved by exploring positive alternatives in this framework of logic, and emotional intelligence. Emotional intelligence is one of the pathways for arriving at positive police leadership solutions.

Travis Bradberry and Jean Greaves, in their book, *Emotional Intelligence, 2.0*, describe the journey to building emotional intelligence. Their book has one purpose: teach others how to build (EQ) abilities. The good news is that leaders can develop emotional intelligence with the proper training. The authors provide an emotional intelligence action plan for building emotional intelligence.

Their research indicates that technically proficient leaders who have a higher EQ perform better than leaders who have a higher Intelligence Quotient (IQ). There are four basic cluster competencies: (1) self-awareness, (2) self-management, (3) social awareness, and (4) relationship management. Emotional intelligence has two components: (1) inner emotional qualities, and (2) other directed personal qualities.

What does this research suggest for police leaders? Positive police leaders should address basic EQ qualities that enhance star performance. According to the above-cited authors, emotional self-awareness describes the ability to engage in accurate self-assessment. Self-management requires emotional self-control. Social awareness requires compassion and an understanding of an officer's daily struggles. The good news is that positive EQ skills can be taught and learned through study and application.

Daniel Goleman wrote his best-selling book, *Emotional Intelligence*, revolutionizing the way we examine human and leadership potential. Early attempts to measure human potential placed emphasis on: The Intelligence Quotient (IQ). The myth of the Intelligence Quotient (IQ) being the key to success was finally put to rest.

According to Reldan S. Nadler's book, *Leading With Emotional Intelligence*, emotional intelligence is the primary influencing factor concerning star performers in the work place. In fact, having one's brains emotionally hijacked reduces problem-solving power and the leader's intelligence quotient or IQ. The problem-solving process demands emotional competencies; both are connected to positive leadership and decision-making.

Cherniss and Goleman's research identified key star performer competencies. This cluster of behaviors is constantly being updated to reflect the current research of what constitutes a star performer. The star performer definition identifies the top 10 percent of successful leaders based on emotional and personal qualities. Emotional intelligence describes leaders who demonstrate a good balance of personal and social competencies in the cited clusters. Refer to the Epilogue for a detailed list of the basic competency clusters.

Star performer leadership requires a persistent and consistent effort. Effective police leaders prepare for future responsibilities through the diligent application of emotional intelligence competencies. This style of leadership starts with timely preparation and follows through on the problem-solving process. This kind of leadership requires confidence, flexibility, and problem-solving skills.

What constitutes a star performer? According to Robert E. Kelley … "A star performer is defined as a person performing in the top 10% of an organization, while average performers make up 60 – 80% of the workforce." His book identifies key competencies that star performers consistently demonstrate. In addition, these basic competencies find direct applications to the field of law enforcement and problem-solving solutions.

Why does emotional intelligence and positive leadership set the foundation for problem-solving solutions? The answer: problem-solving requires a range of social abilities to deploy police operations. Police solutions involve the coordination of problem-solving skills that stem from the combination of critical thinking and EQ. This form of analysis requires accurate information and criminal intelligence. Three major positive leadership pathways emerge: (1) emotional intelligence, (2) positive leadership, and (3) the basic police paradigms.

POLICE PARADIGMS REVIEW

Police paradigms provide the central pathway for meeting the strategic vision, goals, and objectives. The power of the policing paradigm is in the theory and application of ideas. The word paradigm stems from the Greek word paradeigma. The word paradigm means a truth-seeking assumption, theory, and frame of reference, comprising critical thinking, and a prism for viewing complex organizational requirements.

Police leaders, who want to make quantum leaps forward, incorporate policing paradigms as multiple pathways. The ultimate destination for leaders is a sustainable future that anticipates significant events. Policing theories or paradigms evolve rapidly. Police paradigms require the strategic redistribution of traditional police resources. The major police paradigms are: (1) Intelligence-Led Policing (ILP), (2) Community-Oriented Policing (COP), (3) Problem-Oriented Policing (POP), and (4) CompStat.

INTELLIGENCE-LED POLICING (ILP)

Police leaders who possess emotional intelligence listen to the flow of information and seize the initiative. Their actions stem from accurate self-assessment, confidence, and the desire to achieve problem-solving objectives. The information feedback loop includes intelligence information from officers, criminal intelligence, and citizen feedback. Accurate police intelligence provides the central guidance for positive police leaders and their officers to follow.

ILP serves as the criminal information source for strategic and tactical planning. The emphasis is on the intelligence cycle, and sharing criminal information. ILP does not provide strategies to problem-solving solutions. The POP and SARA planning process employ actionable criminal information to deal with underlying crime problem solution(s). Refer to Figure 1-1-B for an illustration of an ILP Definition, Strategies, and Applications.

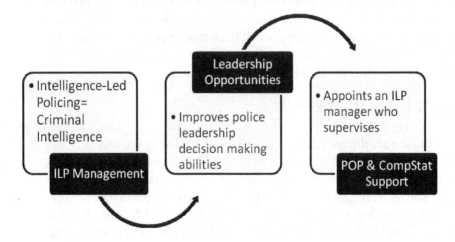

Figure: 1-1-B. ILP Definition, Strategies, and Applications

The United States Department of Justice, Bureau of Justice Assistance identifies the following practices that should be adopted for the successful implementation of ILP strategies:

- Information collection is part of the organizational culture—led by the chief executive, supervisors, and managers who encourage line officers and investigators to regularly collect and forward intelligence.
- Analysis is indispensable to tactical and strategic planning—record management systems are robust, analysts are well-trained and equipped, and actionable intelligence products are regularly produced to inform both tactical and strategic decisions.
- Enforcement tactics are focused, prioritized by community harm assessments and prevention-oriented; operations are

mounted against repeat or violent offenders; serious organized (gang, trafficking, etc.) groups are identified and
dismantled; traffic violations are enforced at dangerous
intersections or roadways.

- Problem-solving principles, community norms, and neighborhood expectations of police service, and resources from
other government, private, and faith-based organizations
are regularly incorporated into law enforcement interventions.
- Privacy is preserved and protected by practices and policies
that are consistent with the ideals of a democratic society.

ILP represents a strategic policing criminal information component. ILP management systems encourage the rapid flow of
criminal information. The timely dissemination of criminal information supports problem-solving and tactical operations. The
intelligence cycle platform and basic components comprise an
interconnected system of services that allow problem-solving
solutions.

The foundation for ILP evolves from intelligence analysis and
crime analysis. Intelligence analysis supports conspiracy and
enterprise crime investigations. The focus is on a systems approach that influences organized crime patterns and their
influence on community. Crime analysis focuses on street serial
crimes that occur in crime hot spots.

The emphasis is on internal intelligence sharing and timely
dissemination with other law enforcement agencies. ILP intelligence requirements support POP strategic and tactical police
operations. Intelligence supports staff studies that directly apply
to the Community-Oriented Policing (COP) and Problem-
Oriented Policing (POP) problem-solving process. Refer to Figure
1-1-C for a brief graphic synopsis of the Intelligence Cycle.

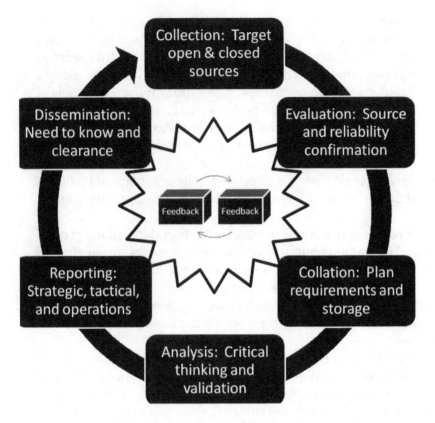

Figure: 1-1-C. Intelligence Cycle

COMMUNITY-ORIENTED POLICING (COP)

Police community leadership acknowledges the role of the community and COP in solving its problems. Diligent leadership and community ownership promote problem-solving solutions. Positive police leadership and excellent police communication have direct applications that benefit communities.

The Community-Oriented Policing philosophy requires community interaction that supports problem-solving solutions. Therefore, positive leadership is a necessary problem-solving component. Positive human relations and emotional intelligence frame the proper social climate for solutions to the crime problems that plague communities.

COP serves as a broader organizational philosophy that builds community partnerships and civic support groups.

Moreover, COP encourages changes in organizational structure. Examples include: decentralized decision-making, fixed community outreach posts, and police training programs that support collaborative problem-solving. COP philosophy benefits will never fully materialize without POP and SARA: Scanning, Analysis, Response, and Assessment planning strategies. COP plus POP and SARA equals COPPS. Refer to Figure 1-2 for an illustration of the COP Definition, Strategies, and Applications.

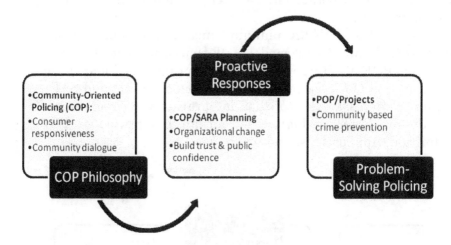

Figure: 1-2. COP Definition, Strategies, and Applications

PROBLEM-SOLVING POLICING (POP)

POP predisposes that logic and reasoning can serve as proactive elements in crime intervention and prevention strategies. Four basic assumptions define POP: (1) crime and disorder can experience reduction through a careful assessment of the problem; (2) police officers then focus on a geographical area and collect crime statistics to arrive at the correct solution; (3) individual offenders make choices based on the opportunities, physical, and social demographics of the crime hot spot; and, (4) responding to the hot spot police services can make a contribution to lowering the fear and level of crime.

According to Goldstein theory, the problem-solving process requires an examination of underlying conditions that create the community crime problem. The analytical process includes examining crime conditions: (1) offenders, (2) victims, and (3) social circumstances structurally conducive to crime. Remedial actions attempt to manipulate these factors to deter, reduce, or eliminate the crime problem.

POP is a concentrated endeavor to resolve the cause of crime, not simply the symptoms of crime. POP incorporates a number of COP goals, including: building partnerships to prevent crime. COP assists in building relationships, cooperation, and trust factors that incorporate citizen participation in the problem-solving process.

The POP and SARA planning models are linked to the strategic ILP intelligence model. POP focuses on crime hotspots; however, POP also targets minor crimes that breed fear in the community. POP is the strategic component of COP, and SARA planning serves as the core for integrating the synchronized paradigms. Refer to Figure 1-3 for an illustration of POP Definition, Applications, and Strategies.

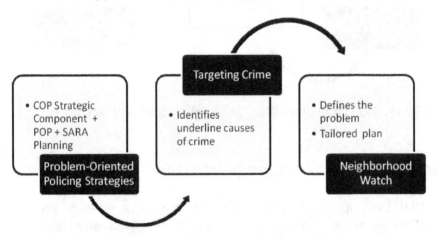

Figure: 1-3. POP Definition, Strategies, and Applications

POP has a long-term view that focuses on community-oriented policing strategies. POP long-term considerations are similar to strategic intelligence analysis: capabilities of criminals and organizations and related community problems. An overlapping planning relationship supports strategic intelligence analysis and POP.

COP differs in the use of citizen strategies such as: community feedback, partnerships, and Neighborhood Watch participation.

POP examines incident-based reporting in the search for broadly based targets. Strategic intelligence involves scanning for broadly based targets.

NEIGHBORHOOD-ORIENTED POLICING (NOP)

Community empowerment leads to effective Neighborhood Watch Programs. Positive police leadership and coordinated neighborhood networks facilitate human trust factors that are converted into community action. Positive police coordination and cooperation pull together neighborhoods and citizen solidarity.

NOP includes a local approach of police and community members working together, and engaged to reduce crime and address the fear of crime through original proactive programs. The Neighborhood Watch program serves as a method to broaden community participation and approach crime block-by-block. NOP is a street component of the COP and POP philosophy that focuses on neighborhood police and citizen interaction and co-operation. The NOP neighborhood approach is not entirely sustainable without COP, POP, and SARA problem-solving components. Refer to Figure 1-4 for an illustration and definition of a NOP Definition, Strategies, and Applications.

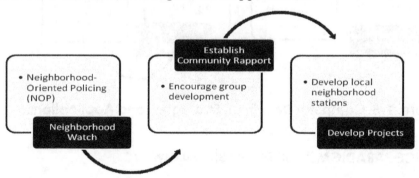

Figure: 1-4. NOP Definition, Strategies and Applications

Community conflict is handled block-by-block and represents a considerable workload requirement for policing. Neighborhood conflict can quickly erupt into violence. Policing is a partnership with the community; addressing group and citizen conflict successfully is important. Officers responding to community conflict understand the leadership, planning, and group dynamics.

The goal of neighborhood policing is the cohesion of community members and individual block-watch programs. Cohesion results in an environment that encourages mutual respect, trust, confidence, understanding, and excellent communication. Social networks in residential areas can organize to protect the neighborhood.

COMPSTAT OPERATIONS

CompStat is not the same as POP; however, the two share some similar components. CompStat statistics generally attack geographic hot spots; however, POP can target the wider foundations and cross-section of crime. POP and CompStat derive strategic criminal information from ILP and the intelligence cycle. Refer to Figure 1-5 for an illustration and definition of the CompStat Definition, Strategies, and Applications.

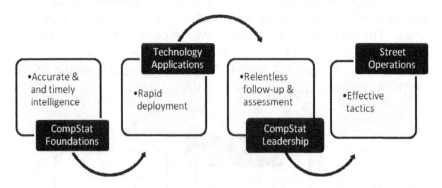

Figure: 1-5. CompStat Definition, Strategies, and Applications

POLICE PARADIGMS: THE TEN BASIC PATHWAYS

In summary, the "Grand Theory" and related policing paradigms are: Intelligence-Led Policing (ILP) + Community-Oriented Policing (COP) + Problem-Oriented Policing (POP) + Neighborhood-Oriented Policing (NOP) + CompStat Tactical Operations (CTO) = Police Excellence (PE). The following ten strategies and pathways form the foundation for supporting these police paradigms:

Strategy One: Positive Police Pathways and Strategies

According to Marilyn Peterson, Intelligence-Led Policing (ILP) represents the new policing architecture that drives police operations. The synchronization of these paradigm strategies offers opportunities that assist in defining where the department is going. The flow of criminal information establishes an important component of the vision forecasting process. Policing is now target specific, rather than random patrol. Refer to Figure 1-6 for an illustration and example of Synchronization Applications.

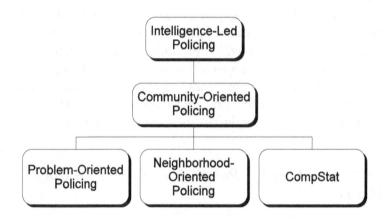

Figure: 1-6. Synchronization of Police Paradigms

Intelligence-Led Policing (ILP) is the primary pathway to effective decision-making. ILP is the management tool for centralizing intelligence criminal information operations. Additional positive leadership pathways include: (1) Community-Oriented Policing (COP), (2) Problem-Oriented Policing (POP), or the combination equals (COPPS), and (3) CompStat. This chapter provides further explanation concerning the synchronization and integration of these related positive pathways.

Strategy Two: Positive Strategic Leadership Strategies

Strategic thinking requires viewing the past retrospectively and peering into the future. Long-term planning requires anticipating events before they take place, thereby, creating a future destination. Strategic thinking requires basic problem-solving analytical tools. Vision allows police leaders to arrive in a timely manner that anticipates the safety of the community, police officers, and citizens.

Successful command problem-solving strategies require building innovative logistical and support systems. Superior commanders encourage sharing excellent ideas and intelligence with everyone in the department. More importantly, positive leaders strategically plan and develop observations that generate solutions to crime and disorder. Strategic planning has the potential to assist commanders in determining: Where is the police department going next?

Leadership is a high-energy quest released for future vision and collective benefits. Positive leadership creates this energy so that police officers may follow. When police leaders release positive energy, officers increase vision understanding. The primary function of positive leadership: create vision energy. The quality and quantity of this collective energy inspires officers; therefore, the energy generated exceeds the original positive leadership source.

Strategy Three: Positive Police Leadership: Finding the Pathway

Commanders, middle managers/leaders, majors, captains, and lieutenants, are movers of change in police organizations. They serve in strategic positions to promote change at their leadership level. Their principal roles represent commanders and coordinators of three specialized functions: (1) patrol, (2) traffic, and (3) investigative. Lieutenants may serve as watch commanders or command specialized units, including: special POP projects.

The POP strategy: empower officers and set the foundation for a team effort. Team leadership is at the core of excellent police POP strategies and tactics. Creating competent teams creates higher level performance than officers standing alone. Police team leaders seek new ways to use officer abilities and team talents.

Teamwork requires that positive police leaders give respect and officers respect each other. Police team members (officers) must share a common bond that supports organizational membership. Officers trust and depend on each member of the team; therefore, they aspire to team expectations. Officers share a commitment to the team rather than individual success.

Proactive leadership principles encourage focus and attention on the overarching vision, providing motivation and hope for a better future. Astute leaders express the vision in a hopeful and consistent manner; this encourages officers and civilians to enhance the vision. Officers begin to envision their own alliance and contribution by following pathways to vision success. Vision and energy provide the motivational pathway for officers and civilians to follow.

Strategy Four: Positive Motivational Leadership: Finding the Way

Police leaders who perform at the maximum level of their abilities motivate officers to follow. Positive leaders inspire officers by demonstrating commitment to the department's mission and goals. Police leaders who "take care of their officers" shape a positive social climate. Positive police leadership requires insight into officer motivation and community point of view.

High quality leadership is in the best position to set elevated standards and achieve maximum effort from their officers. Leaders, who set the example and demonstrate the correct behaviors and enthusiasm, will motivate officers. Police officers will adopt similar attitudes and mirror positive leadership behaviors.

Leaders who successfully show concern for the development of their officers or civilians mentor well. Excellent problem-solving behaviors should be praised; police officers need recognition and approval. Both represent powerful incentives. Police officers who take pride in their work exert the maximum motivational effort in the areas of POP problem-solving solutions. Insightful police leaders provide positive psychology foundations, motivation and direction.

Leaders, who understand how to motivate their officers, make them aware that personal qualities can make a contribution. Positive leaders tell officers and civilians that they have the potential to make a difference. Unique attributes can help achieve the mission and future vision.

Strategy Five: Positive Problem-solving Communication

Positive leadership is accomplished through consistent and persistent communication, which demonstrates integrity and trust. When communication happens, officers feel valued and compelled to follow. The leader searches for positive communication connections and bonds that lead to goal accomplishment. Moreover, communication foundations increase problem-solving participation. Police leaders serve as mentors and guideposts for their officers.

Positive messages and impressions are created when using powerful communication. Officers attempt to understand and are ready to take action on their leader's suggestions and thoughts. Positive leadership starts with communicating and leading from the community and officer perspective.

Officer-oriented leadership demonstrates competence and transparency that assures rapport and communication. The vision is clearly defined, if the police leader is going to achieve success. Rapport-oriented leaders know how to communicate so their officers may follow. Essential police messages persuade officers toward higher levels of performance, enthusiasm, and outstanding team procedures.

Strategy Six: Positive Problem-solving Training

Training for problem-oriented policing involves: (1) coaching and (2) teaching. The Chief of Police and senior leaders are ultimately responsible for guiding the department's problem-solving training program. Training and teaching occurs at every level of the police department. Individual officers become coaches and trainers; cross-training unfolds systematically.

Positive police mentoring encourages officers to train for success. Generally, "problem-solving" leaders serve in a position to provide on-the-job skill development and excellent training assignments. Most importantly, problem-solving leaders encourage positive achievement, and promote the success and reputation of their officers.

Positive training and teaching strategies provide the road to success. Successful police departments are built on the exchange of ideas and the ability to clarify those ideas. Problem-solving training provides new ways of examining community crime issues. Leaders coach, teach, and instill the necessary discipline to reach those goals. Every member of the department becomes a teacher when they share their expertise and knowledge.

Strategy Seven: Positive Strategic Planning, Evaluation & Assessment

Police senior leaders look further into the future than their subordinates. The success of any organization depends on the ability to forecast the future. Senior leaders envision what needs to be accomplished and influence subordinates to complete related goals. The vision statement is the thoughtful, future analysis, and planning that enables leaders to develop a system that attempts to forecast the future.

Strategic leaders provide the future pathway through planning and positive guidance. This form of planning requires vision that extends far into the future. While one cannot absolutely predict the future, trends can reveal critical information about the general destination. The strategic plan includes a description of the police department's long-term goals and related objectives. The general strategy provides a statement regarding how to accomplish defined goals and objectives. In addition, the action plan describes how to reach that destination.

Strategy Eight: Positive SARA Planning

Well-formulated POP planning, problem-solving policies, and procedures provide guidance for officers. Positive POP planning provides direction for officers, without confusion or delay. Police officers have to accomplish much of their own planning, when plans are not well developed.

Police Department Intervention Steps:

Step #1: Identify the problems.
Step #2: Recognize and define correct behaviors.
Step #3: Identify distinct patterns of crime.
Step #4: Develop a constructive solution to the existing related problems.
Step #5: Assessment and Evaluation

Police commanders make constructive judgments about the results after the analysis phase. Analysis includes searching for meaning and finding trends and patterns. This means determining how to interpret the data and developing applications that might be useful to the police organization and community. When officers develop excellent SARA planning and procedures, they follow the protocols, thereby requiring less supervision. Police leaders select the methods that produce accurate SARA planning results. Excellent SARA planning requires less frequent police leadership guidance and excessive officer time for consultation.

Strategy Nine: Positive Problem-solving: Pop Projects

Police officers are problem-solvers and decision-makers. As a group, police officers probably make more independent decisions than their commanders on a daily basis. In critical incident scenarios, life and death decisions are made without consulting supervisors or commanders. Absolute control over police officers is highly improbable. However, POP projects offer leaders opportunities to provide influence in the decision-making process.

POP Project leaders/managers give direction to officers on how to improve their POP project skills, avoid mistakes, and provide assistance in technical problem-solving. POP project leaders allow their officers to problem-solve rather than offer obvious solutions. Trust and expressive support may be more important than POP information and guidance.

Strategy Ten: Positive Coaching: Police Operations

Coaching is the best method for improving police performance. The coaching process involves examining performance and providing information on improvement. Positive police leaders seek to motivate and support professional development. They coach and train their officers for developing POP expertise. The police leader's primary responsibility is to assist POP teams in the journey to reach their potential.

The coach starts the officer on the simple tasks first, which increases confidence, and achievement. Officers improve decision-making and openness to the changing requirements. The effective coach monitors progress, and rewards POP performance improvement.

A problem-solving coach evaluates officers, recognizing talent and potential. They are usually more experienced; however, coaching may come from the same peer and team level. One does not need rank to coach; however, it requires time, energy, communication abilities, and accurate feedback. Police coaches might also serve as professional mentors, and advisors. There is a higher and better way when coaches and mentors support officers in the problem-oriented policing strategies.

FOCUS POINTS

Positive leaders bring forth hope for the future and support their staff and police teams through periods of adversity. When officers and civilians become overwhelmed by enormous energy requirements, superior police leaders provide support and direction. Thoughtful police leaders know how to remain positive in the face of adversity. Star police performers instill confidence and the desire to move forward on goals and objectives.

Emotional intelligence is essential to successful police work and positive relationships with other officers. Emotional intelligence and self-control is more important than general intelligence when leading and managing police officers. The application of these emotional skills requires being open, candid, and the ability to maintain professional relationships.

Effective police leadership requires interacting successfully with officers, building relationships, and then working toward personal and professional goals. Exceptional police leaders inspire their officers to attempt to do things they never thought they could accomplish on their own. They never forget how it felt to be an officer and experience the benefits of positive leadership.

Affirmative leadership requires a blend of appropriate consideration and positive discipline. Officers require guidance; moreover, they benefit from empowerment to fulfill POP problem-solving requirements. Police leaders provide some structure; however, they do not dictate how to accomplish field problem-solving.

The philosophy of community-oriented policing is part of the fabric of American policing. COP focus is on community members and civic groups to solve specific underlying crime problems. COP fundamental ambitions are reducing the fear and level of crime. Citizen involvement is a central tenant of the COP paradigm.

COP is a philosophy, not a particular program; it is flexible and adaptable to communities. The goal of COP is to solve crime problems that concern neighborhoods and communities. The police and members of the community share crime-fighting responsibilities through cooperation in the problem-solving process.

COP analyzes specific crime problems and builds external partnerships. POP, the strategic arm of COP, provides the framework for problem-solving. POP problem-solving strategies focus on crime generators and hot spots, which threaten communities. The planning process incorporates POP and SARA strategies to realize COP philosophy goals and objectives.

Positive police leaders understand that mutual respect improves thoughtful and creative thinking. The most important attributes of POP leadership and planning: (1) give officers ownership for the problem, (2) encourage critical thinking and problem-solving, (3) facilitate and support excellent initiatives and creative ideas, and (4) credit and reward officers who make meaningful contributions.

Evaluators obtain information that guides police leaders in the decision-making process. The evaluation/assessment process reduces uncertainty and assists officers and citizens in crime reduction. Research methods must be accurate and assist in developing future planning requirements. The evaluation/assessment process permits police leaders to determine if the department has arrived and define future destinations.

CONCLUSION

Policing strategies overlap and interconnect, making classification difficult. In addition, law enforcement professionals may apply terminology interchangeably. Diverse localities and professional advocates of one paradigm may borrow ideas and concepts from another. New variations of police paradigms appear under various terminology, nomenclature, and modifications. For example, another new paradigm, predictive policing, practices some of the proactive strategies stated in this chapter.

Finally, policing paradigms also provide guidance for police officers to anticipate department direction. Policing requires considerable thought about community requirements that support quality service. Police paradigms provide the management system for preventing, suppressing, and prosecuting criminal behavior.

CHAPTER 2
POSITIVE POLICE STRATEGIC LEADERSHIP STRATEGIES

"A relatively small number of individuals usually account for a disproportionate share of practically any problem the police handle. Police have long been alert to the phenomenon of the one-man crime wave."
— Herman Goldstein

Creating a high performance police organization is defined by strategic leadership. Strategic leadership should facilitate the mission statement, core values, and behaviors that reflect excellent performance. The strategic mission statement describes and anticipates future requirements. The positive police leader describes the vision for reaching new destinations and provides the inspirational voice for the future.

In his book entitled, *The 8th Habit: From Effectiveness to Greatness*, Stephen R. Covey comments: "Find your voice and inspire others to find theirs. Voice lies at the nexus of talent (your natural gifts and strengths), passion (those things that naturally energize, excite, motivate and inspire you), and conscience (that still, small voice within that assures you of what is right and prompts you to actually do it)."

CHAPTER FOCUS

Strategic decision-making requires department reorganization and the manner in which police agencies anticipate the future. This chapter describes the role of strategic leadership in sharing vision, strategic goals, and objectives. Strategic leaders describe their vision of police agency destinations.

OVERVIEW: STRATEGIC LEADERSHIP

Senior leaders and mid-level leaders represent primary initiators of strategic change, administration, and coordination functions. Strategic leaders are initiators of organizational change and are concerned with the physical and human resources required to improve strategic and maximum performance. The aim of reorganizational structure is to enable a group of officers to function as a unit, without interference or effort duplication.

Police reorganization is the primary way to demonstrate a commitment to the future. Police strategic leadership focuses on potential opportunities for providing superior police service. Positive police leadership and balanced team building provide the strategic picture. The Tampa Police Department serves as a model for initiating strategic reorganization.

POLICE STAR LEADERSHIP PERFORMERS

Positive police leadership and emotional intelligence (EQ) have similar aspects and combine to enhance human potential. Emotional intelligence embraces effective self awareness and self-management of the positive police leader's own emotions. This form of self-management provides the foundation for managing police officers and civilians.

Emotional intelligence sets the example for police officers to follow and embraces four basic foundations: (1) understanding yourself, (2) defining your goals, (3) stating your intentions, and (4) developing insightful responses. These strategic efforts require understanding the needs of your officers and civilians, in particular, respecting their feelings.

Formulating accurate assumptions allows officers to construct a consistent framework that ensures working toward similar goals and objectives. The learning process encourages debate, ideas, and the emotional intelligence to pursue the mission. Positive leadership expedites the emotional intelligence process and necessary changes in rapidly changing police organizations and community environments.

TELLING THE STORY: LEADING OFFICERS

Telling the personal story offers an opportunity to define the future destination. Police leadership provides the vision and values to pursue the mission. Telling the story is the primary means to target the problem for analysis and POP solutions. Describing the problem sets the foundation for the strategic mission. Effective senior and middle police leadership guides officers to the correct solutions by providing adequate structure and support.

Supportive police cultures and organizations create trusting environments that ensure high morale and motivation. Defining winning pathways requires consistent storylines that encourage application of emotional intelligence. Howard Garner, in his book, *Leading Minds*, notes that people learn from illustrative stories.

Garner identifies three major storylines that leaders have used successfully throughout history.

Who am I?: Personal storylines that explain the history of the leader and how life experiences have shaped the leader's point of view.

Who are we?: Storylines that demonstrate joint experiences, attitudes, values, and beliefs that shape and form the basis for a shared point of view.

Where are we going?: Storylines that capture the necessity for change. Moreover, the leader creates excitement about future direction and destinations.

Positive leaders provide pathways using three storylines. They describe what is special about their police agency, and essential team performance. Gardner defines future destinations that answer the question: Where are we going? He explores three basic components:

The case for change: Why does the team or police organization need to change?

Where are we going?: What is the strategic picture for the police agency in the future?

How will we get there?: What necessary steps will every officer in the police organization take to achieve the vision? Why should officers and civilians have confidence that the vision can be accomplished?

STRATEGIC DECISION-MAKING

Strategic decision-making evolves as sequence of lesser decisions and choices among alternatives. Analyzing past mistakes builds a successful bridge to the future. This is accomplished through planning and research that is presented at staff meet-

ings. In most cases, the commander supports staff recommendations and decisions. Police leaders develop staff studies that
target criminal activities and assess results. In addition, leaders
and officers remain steadfast and relentless in their pursuit of
criminal activity.

Problem-solving does not imply delegating leadership power
without guidance. Leaders who distribute power and authority
also share: vision, values, and goals for others to follow. The
POP strategy requires communication, and providing structure
throughout the police organization. Superior leadership may
require the opposite of what appears to be common sense, or
differs from conventional thinking.

Goals and objectives define strategic priorities. Police leaders
constantly review and obtain feedback from officers and
community stakeholders to modify strategic plans. Information
is garnered for future modification of the emerging changes
in the fear and level of crime. Regular intelligence feedback
provides police agencies with positive community responses.

CRIMINAL INTELLIGENCE: THE STRATEGIC PICTURE

The Intelligence Cycle and criminal information provides
senior commanders, middle leaders, and supervisors with crime
patterns and hot spot locations. Criminal information concerning
offenses permits targeting strategies and tactics. Criminal
information is passed on to shift commanders and patrol sergeants for tactical applications.

The Criminal Intelligence Cycle is the primary means for
detecting, obtaining, and confirming feedback from the intricate
workings of the criminal world. Three basic Criminal Intelligence
Cycle steps include: (1) define intelligence problem requirements,
(2) identify the target(s), (3) define the collection plan, (4) conduct
analysis, and (5) provide the proper information dissemination.
The intelligence cycle, planning, and targeting, incorporate an
ongoing cycle through multiple feedback loops. Refer to Figure
2-1 for an example of the Intelligence Cycle, Threat and Risk
Assessment Analysis.

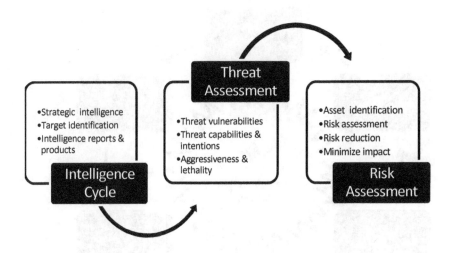

Figure: 2-1 Intelligence Cycle, Threat and Risk Assessment

After identifying the target(s) through the intelligence gathering process, patrol allocation decides how many officers are needed in a particular target, hot spot area, and sector. The intelligence cycle and targeting assignments provide the means to address community needs and the personnel power to support police services. Allocation decisions concern geographical targets, calls for service, department goals, and objectives. The strategic ILP destination focuses on intelligence clarity that is necessary for target planning. Once leaders collect the necessary criminal information, opportunities for successful direction and mission accomplishment emerge. Refer to Figure 2-2 for an illustration of the Intelligence Cycle Targeting and related targets.

Problem-solving policing requires gathering accurate and actionable criminal information. This is accomplished through collection, analysis, planning, and targeting the underlying community problems. After defining the target(s) and describing problem requirements, the most important task is the timely dissemination of the criminal information to field operating units.

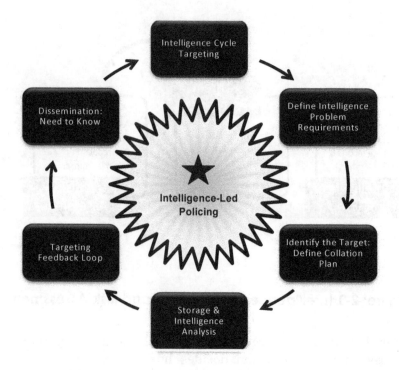

Figure: 2-2. Intelligence Cycle Targeting

The combination of accurate intelligence/crime analysis leads to the identification of hot spots or clusters of crime. Crime analysis and crime specific planning provide opportunities for prevention and intervention targeting. This attention or primary focus identifies a specific area that has a high rate of offending for serial offenses.

The strategy suggests that a small number of addresses, places, offenders, or combination thereof, require special responses. The hot spot can generate significantly higher and unrelenting demands for calls for service. One way to frame the problem scope is to "Tell the Story." Examine the following Problem-Solving Corner for the basic mechanism.

PROBLEM-SOLVING CORNER: TELLING THE STORY

Clarke and Eck describe the storytelling process: "A framework is a general 'story shell' linking multiple interacting actors that can be applied to a variety of problems. Your choice of frameworks depends on the problem, your findings, and the needs of decision-makers. Be sure there is a logical flow from the basic question, through the framework and findings, to the answers. Check for gaps in logic. Now outline your story. There are four basic story outlines that can guide your work. The details of the story will depend on the specifics of the problem.

Do not stick religiously to these outlines; they are a starting point to prompt ideas. Instead, tailor them to the amount of time available and, above all, to the concerns of the people whom you are addressing. Try to anticipate their questions and modify the appropriate outline accordingly. If your audience is not already familiar with the terminology of problem analysis, you probably should use it sparingly, or not at all.

Four Story Outlines

1. *What is the nature of the problem?*
   a. Organize a framework for the problem.
   b. Systematic description of evidence about problem type and existence:
   - What is the nature of the events?
   - In what ways are these events similar?
   - How often do these events recur?
   - When and where do these events occur?
   - Who is harmed by these events, and how?
   - Who expects the police to address the problem?
   - Implications for analysis and collaborative problem solving:
   - Questions that need answering.
   - Definitional and measurement issues.
   - Partners who need to become involved.

2. *What causes the problem?*
   a. Organizing framework for problem—for example, problem analysis triangle.
   b. Systematic description of the problem that answers the following questions:
   - Who are the offenders?
   - Who or what are the targets?
   - At what places and times does the problem occur?

- What brings the offenders and targets together at the same places?
- Why don't other problem-solving steps prevent these encounters?
- What facilitates or inhibits the problem?

3. *What should be done about this problem?*
   a. Organizing framework for response—for example, situational crime prevention:
      - Offenders
      - Targets/victims
      - Places
   b. Systematic description of response strategy:
      - Increasing risk or effort.
      - Decreasing reward, excuses, or provocations.
      - Who will carry out actions, when, and where?
      - Additional resources required.
   c. Implications and anticipated outcomes:
      - Direct results.
      - Displacement.
      - Diffusion.
      - Other side effects.
      - How evaluation should be conducted?
   d. Summary

4. *How the response reduced the problem?*
   a. Organizing framework—for example, principles of evaluation
   b. Systematic description of evaluation:
      - Was the response implemented as planned?
      - Did the problem change?
      - Why it is likely that the response was a direct cause of change.
      - The magnitude of displacement, diffusion, and other side effects.
   c. Implications for further action.
      - Is this problem-solving effort complete?
      - What further actions are necessary?
      - Should further analysis be conducted?
      - Should the response be changed?
   d. Summary"

Source: R. V. Clarke and J. E. Eck, *Crime Analysis for Problem-Solvers: In 60 Small Steps*, U.S. Dept. of Justice: Community Oriented Policing Services (COPS) (Washington DC: GPO, 2005): 46.

PROBLEM-SOLVING CORNER: TAMPA POLICE DEPARTMENT

The Tampa Police Department Problem-Solving Corner serves as an excellent example of the strategic thinking process. Intelligence-led policing builds foundations, while maintaining a community-oriented approach. The Tampa Police Department realized that partnering with the community offered an important police benefit. The following Problem-Solving Corner describes how the Tampa Police Department redesigned its mission statement and made futuristic changes that improved policing services.

Focus on Four: Jane Castor, Chief of Police, Marc Hamlin, Assistant Chief, and John Bennett, Assistant Chief, implemented a new vision and destination for the Tampa Police Department. The Tampa Police Department's POP strategies focus on The Big Four crime problems. Their strategic plan targeted high volume crimes that plagued the community of 333,040 citizens and 992 police officers. Targeted responses dramatically reduced crime. Strategies based on ILP and crime statistics mirror the Comp-Stat tactics approach. The results are impressive, crime rate overall down 56%: burglary 44.2%, robbery 61%, auto burglary 59.9%, and auto theft 79%.

Intelligence-Led Policing

The first step in launching Intelligence-Led Policing crime fighting was to reconfigure the department's records system to create a data warehouse. This step enabled crime analysts to easily access data and produce daily reports for the districts. These reports detailed crimes committed in a 24-hour period and compared each day's crimes to the previous month and to the same month from the prior year. Supervisors closely followed and targeted The Big Four volume crimes: (1) burglary, (2) robbery, (3) automobile burglary, and (4) automobile theft. These offenses accounted for the majority of crimes committed. Success was evaluated based on the crime rate reduction for that month, as compared to the same month the prior year.

Tracking offenses as they occurred became a critical element of the department's new crime reduction tactics. It allowed the district majors to deploy the newly decentralized resources to attack emerging crime patterns and trends as urgently as possible. To provide this real-time intelligence information, the department formed the Crime Analysis Unit, and assigned each district an analyst. A daily analytical report was created that identified when, how, and where the crimes were being committed, and who the likely offenders were. This information allowed for a more efficient and effective deployment of resources.

Computer mapping of crime data was completed on a weekly and monthly basis. Commanders and officers easily determined where crimes were being committed geographically and were able to utilize the information from these maps to assist in decision-making and strategies.

To ensure the highest level of accountability, the Tampa Police Department instituted a monthly review process termed: The Comprehensive Police Performance Effectiveness Review or COPPER for short. The COPPER reports contained high-level details on all crime and related responses for each district. The Assistant Chief of Operations reviewed these reports at monthly COPPER meetings.

This action allowed for a department-wide review and analysis to ensure each district was doing its part to effectively reduce crime. In essence, they became the report card for district commanders and their staff. This paradigm shift of expecting officers and police commanders to proactively reduce crime often created a highly charged atmosphere at the COPPER meetings.

Simplify the Mission

The mission statement needed to be simple enough for the entire department and community to: understand, internalize, and embrace. As a result, a simple and direct mission statement was developed focusing on crime reduction. This mission statement became ingrained in every aspect of the department and developed into a guiding principle. It established measurable crime reduction as the basic tenant of the administration.

"The mission of the Tampa Police Department is to reduce crime and improve the quality of life through a cooperative partnership with all citizens."

Partnering with the Community

The Department's Community Oriented Policing philosophy established and maintained an open line of communication and mutual trust with the community. These positive relationships continue to be a cornerstone of the department's crime reduction success. By virtue of partnerships with the community, the Department's mission of crime reduction became the community's mission as well.

Officers were tasked with identifying the needs and concerns of those living or working in the areas they patrolled. The benefit of these relationships could be seen in every neighborhood. They took the form of citizens riding with officers to address prostitution in their neighborhood, calls reporting suspicious activity that led to arrests for property crimes, and roll calls held in residents' front yards. It became rare to find someone in an actively involved neighborhood who didn't know the names of officers who patrolled their area.

An integral part of the Community Oriented Policing was Neighborhood Watch. After all, who knows a neighborhood better than those who live and work there? The Department counted on citizens to truly act as the eyes and ears of the community. Collaboration with residents, Neighborhood Watch members, civic association groups, business partners, and neighborhood mobile patrols were critical to the Department's crime reduction success. Another benefit: when media stories focus on police actions, established relationships with neighborhood leaders help to balance the community's perspective.

As part of the reorganization, the Neighborhood Affairs Liaisons were decentralized and assigned to each district. Instead of having limited contact with the community through monthly meetings, these employees became part of the "front line" of each district's day-to-day operations. Websites and email trees were used to send real-time information. Crime prevention tips, crime alerts, and arrest information were consistently emailed.

The Public Information Office created an external publication that was sent to the community, and posted on the city's web site. The publication highlighted what the Department was doing to keep the community safe. It also educated citizens on how they could get involved in the Department's daily efforts to improve their neighborhoods. The publication was downloaded over

50,000 times in its first year online. This constant communication and combined effort became essential in efforts to reduce crime.

Citizen and police interaction can truly be described as a "team effort." The community shared in both celebrating successes, and shouldering responsibility for areas that still need improvement. We must not forget that we all have a duty to help reduce crime ... neighborhood by neighborhood.

Redistribution of Tactical Resources

To hold officers and supervisors accountable for crime, the administration took steps to ensure that everyone had all the tools necessary to combat crime. It began by dividing the city into three smaller, more manageable districts. Then, as part of the reorganization process, specialized resources were moved out of central police headquarters and redistributed to the districts. These resources included street level drug squads known as QUAD.

QUAD (Quick Uniform Attack on Drugs) and pattern crime squads known as **SAC** (Street Anti-Crime) improved deployment operations. The Department eventually combined these plain clothes squads to create ROC Squads (Rapid Offender Control Squads), assigned to each district. The executive staff slowly expanded decentralization to include: auto theft, robbery, and economic crimes. Detectives, school resource officers, and neighborhood liaisons proved effective. Assigning these officers and employees to the districts allowed each to become its own autonomous police station. The Majors would deploy officers as they saw necessary to combat unique district issues.

The officers and employees also adopted a more proactive and urgent approach to policing. Using a "swarm" mentality, all available units would respond to in-progress calls to increase the chance of capturing the suspect and preventing future crimes. In addition, most offenses were investigated from start to finish at the time of the initial report. Very few cases were referred to a detective for latent investigation.

The decentralization of resources also placed officers and employees in close proximity to the citizens they served. This allowed the formation of intimate working relationships, and a firsthand knowledge of the issues in the assigned geographic areas of responsibility. To effectively combat crime, the district Majors began closely monitoring the Uniform Crime Report (UCR).

The yearly crime report of all cities is derived from the UCR. This report was developed by the FBI in 1930, as a way of standardizing jurisdictional crime measurements throughout the nation. The UCR tracks seven crimes that include: (1) murder, (2) rape, (3) robbery, (4) aggravated assault, (5) larceny-theft, (6) auto theft, and (7) burglary. Statutes and crime definitions vary from state to state.

UCR is the mechanism by which the national reporting is standardized. An essential performance measure of the Focus on Four required planning. The plan was accurate reporting of crime in Tampa. Internal reporting guidelines were fine-tuned and all supervisors received in-depth training. This training ensured crime was reported by correct UCR standards.

The plan primarily targeted four volume crimes: burglary, robbery, automobile burglary, and automobile theft. While the reduction of those crimes alone had a dramatic impact on the community, the ripple effect of catching those criminals profoundly reduced the more violent crimes. Historical crime analysis shows that people who commit more violent crimes also commit a large percentage of the Big Four Crimes. Focusing on the Big Four Crimes for pattern crimes indirectly reduced the overall crime rate 56% over the past seven years.

Once a clear and simple mission was developed, district commanders were assigned all the resources necessary to combat crime in their area. Each district major received real-time intelligence to deploy their resources effectively; thereby, raising the level of accountability at all levels of the organization. A department-wide cultural shift from only responding to 911 calls to a new, proactive approach energized the officers. As they saw their efforts making a difference, enthusiasm and morale grew. A sense of urgency permeated every call, even the most minor of crimes. That momentum prompted officers to develop initiatives to address crime problems specific to their assigned areas. The response was overwhelming. Listed below are a few of the countless successful initiatives.

Rapid Offender Control Squad

Rapid Offender Control Officers, known as ROC, focus on high crime areas called Offender Control Zones. They are armed with intelligence about repeat offenders and crime patterns in their zones so they can more rapidly identify suspects, solve crimes, and prevent additional crimes from occurring. These officers immediately begin the follow-up investigation, in concert with Patrol, before a detective is assigned to a case.

One ROC Officer works in every Offender Control Zone around the clock. The crime problems of each hot zone determine if ROC officers focus on street level narcotics, burglaries, prostitution, robberies, or other crimes. A tactical lieutenant oversees the day-to-day crime patterns and deployment of the ROC officers. They coordinate between Patrol and District Detective Squads to ensure all entities are sharing intelligence and working together to address crime patterns. This supervisor also serves as a key point of contact for citizens, which has enhanced working relationships with the community.

RAT Attack

Over the past seven years, auto thefts in the city have dropped 79.7%. In 2002, stolen vehicles reached an unacceptable high of 6,720 vehicles. By 2009, that number declined to 1,361. Because of the Department's efforts, there are 5,359 less auto theft victims. Crime analysis showed juveniles or young adults stole the majority of the vehicles, often to use in other crimes. The goal: reduce auto thefts while limiting pursuits as much as possible. As a result, the Reduce Auto Theft Program (RAT) was established. Crime analysts identified juveniles who were known auto thieves and mapped the areas around their homes for stolen and recovered autos.

Each recovered stolen car was thoroughly processed for prints and the MO, modus operandi, noted. Analytical information was provided to officers weekly: (1) suspect photos, (2) locations, (3) wanted information, (4) patterns, and (5) any other useful information. Supervisors utilized the Street Anti-Crime Squads to focus intently on auto theft, through surveillance. They would patrol in unmarked vehicles with a computer, running tags of suspect vehicles.

When a stolen car was located, they would coordinate a "box in" technique that would allow apprehension without a pursuit. Word spread fast that it was not just marked units looking for stolen cars. To ensure charges were not dropped, officers transported suspects to court to face prosecution. Street officers then enforced court-ordered curfews and house arrests on juveniles convicted of auto theft. As the auto theft numbers dropped, so did associated auto burglaries.

School's Out — Zero Tolerance

Crime analysis indicated that crime increased during the summer months when school was out. After seven years of these initiatives, summer crime is down 51% in Tampa. Each of the three districts formulated plans that would attack crimes committed by juveniles. Analytical information provided the times, locations, types, and patterns of juvenile crime. Grant funding was utilized to provide extra patrols at the appropriate times and places.

School Resource Officers were placed in the high crime areas to provide historical knowledge of the law breakers. Reassigned resources were placed in those locations with a target-rich environment, such as malls, hotels, and tourist attractions. Each year, a new plan was constructed using the formula of who, what, when, where, and how of the previous summer.

The summer initiatives were kicked off in each district with a positive event that included: (1) a job fair, (2) life skill instruction, (3) food, and (4) games. Everyone was made aware of positive alternatives through Parks and Recreation Programs, and private partnerships. They were also reminded of the police department's zero tolerance on juvenile crime. The crime rate during the summer months declined every year from 2002 to 2009.

Operation Safe Shopper

Innovative operations cut holiday crime 61% in the shopping areas. Each year, crime spiked in the shopping corridors during the holidays and summer breaks. To combat this rise in crime, Tampa Police found new ways to fight old crime through innovative operations. Officers on horseback, motorcycles, bikes, and unmarked vehicles saturated the mall parking lots to prevent auto burglaries, auto thefts, and robberies.

School Resource Officers were utilized to identify those juveniles on mall property who were committing property crimes. The Tampa Police Department provided common sense crime prevention tips through a media blitz. Crime Prevention officers also placed personalized flyers on cars, informing owners of items left in plain view, which would tempt a criminal. The objective was twofold: to educate citizens on how to avoid becoming a victim of crime, and to send a strong message to the criminals on the increased police presence.

Strategic Investigations Bureau

The Tampa Police Department's new approach to narcotic investigations has resulted in the dismantling of 27 drug trafficking organizations and disbanded 39 drug distribution cells. The Narcotics Bureau that targeted upper level drug traffickers citywide, coordinated its efforts with the street level drug squads known as QUAD (Quick Uniform Attack on Drugs) starting in 2004. Through citizen complaints, officers identified areas known for "open air" drug sales, or areas where drug sales fueled other crimes.

QUAD Squads identified those responsible for the street level sales; the Narcotics Squads ascertained and targeted the upper management of suppliers to those street dealers. QUAD Squads conducted routine street buys and made arrests, while co-ordinating intelligence with the Narcotics Squads. The Narcotics Unit often employed Title III Wire Intercepts, referred to as wiretaps, in these investigations. This identified and secured criminal charges on the entire organization that supplied the street level dealers.

Consequently, the police investigation dismantled the entire organization and eliminated the source of the problem, including the main supplier, mid-management, and street dealers. This strategy had the benefit of immediately stopping the drug sales and removing a large criminal element from the neighborhood. These operations often led to other suppliers and organizations affecting the city. These investigations cleaned-up the neigh-borhoods for citizens and solidified partnerships between the police and community.

Diverting Juveniles from Committing Crimes

When analyzing repeat offenders, the Tampa Police Department found that while juveniles do not commit the majority of crimes, a significant percentage of juveniles were committing an inordinate number of offenses. Most of these offenses comprised the Big Four: auto theft, robbery, burglary, and auto burglary. A determination was made that the crime rate could be impacted by targeting these juveniles and diverting them from a life of crime, to constructive programs that would set them on the right track. In 2005, the Tampa Police Department began the Worst of the Worst Initiative, known as WOW. This program targeted juveniles who had lengthy arrest records.

When convicted of a property crime, juveniles were placed on sanctions, as opposed to adult probation. Disobeying these sanctions was an administrative and not a criminal violation, thus there was no additional punishment. It was found that juveniles arrested for auto theft would not show up for court, as there were no consequences. After a few continuances, the victim would give up and the charge would be dropped. An agreement with the court system allowed officers to receive notification of court dates, so officers could take proactive action and transport the juveniles to court and ensure their attendance.

Juvenile Fast Track

The police department also worked to create a fast track in the court system, for repeat juvenile offenders. Chief Castor met with juvenile judges, the State Attorney, Public Defender, and the Juvenile Assessment Center to establish a system that ensured a habitual juvenile offender cases were resolved within 21 days. This allowed the juvenile to face swift consequences, while also being provided with social services to help steer them away from a life of crime. This program has cut down on the revolving door of juveniles being repeatedly arrested without facing a penalty or getting help. Research indicated that most juveniles receiving sanctions had a curfew that no one was enforcing.

Zone officers were assigned to check on the WOW juveniles within their zones. Then they transported anyone violating the curfew to the Juvenile Assessment Center. If school attendance was part of the sanctions, School Resource Officers were assigned to check on the juveniles daily. There was also a heavy focus on truancy. Keeping the students attending school resulted in crime reduction in and around the schools. As a result of the focus on these juveniles, property crimes dropped dramatically, specifically auto thefts and auto burglaries.

This strongly suggested that if there was oversight and consequences for committing crimes, some criminally inclined juveniles would avoid illegal activity. Based on the success of the WOW initiative, Tampa began focusing on those adults who commit large numbers of big four crimes.*

The Tampa Police Department's solutions offer insight for the need to conduct a department wide review of strategies. Leadership clarity requires: (1) the application ILP strategic strategies, (2) partnering with the community, (3) simplifying the mission requirements, (4) defining the new mission statement, (5) applying COP, POP, and neighborhood policing, and finally, (6) clarifying the Big Four Crime Problems.

The Tampa Police Department is an illustration of high-leverage crime fighting strategies based on the Big Four focus points: (1) burglary, (2) robbery, (3) automobile burglary, and (4) automobile theft. This change is a positive example of finding the correct pathway with clarity.

FOCUS POINTS

ILP provides intelligence information for developing strategic targets. Criminal information and hot spot locations provide the basis for POP remedial actions. Intelligence information assists in developing community resources and crime prevention initiatives.

Strategic leaders create and develop social networks beyond their police organization. Social networks in the community include: (1) police partners, (2) clients, and (3) citizens. Simplifying the mission and tailoring goals and objectives benefit crime prevention and suppression.

Strategic leaders set goals, establish procedures, organize, and control police reorganizational programming. In addition, strategic leaders set operational priorities. They authorize the

---

*Source: By permission of the Tampa Police Department.

use of expenditures, track crime, and community conditions. Strategic leaders analyze crime, arrests, and other productivity statistics.

Police leaders were specific about empowering officers and developing clear goals and objectives. The Tampa Police Department's willingness to break-out of their organizational "comfort zone" and engage in controlled change served a noble purpose.

The officers had an unobstructed view of the vision, and understood the mission. Officers could define what their leaders wanted to happen and why it was necessary. The new strategic mission had value to the Tampa Police Department and the community. The mission purpose and values enlisted broad support. Tampa police leaders provided the pathway to successful accomplishment of their goals and objectives.

The establishment of the goals and objectives were tied to the Department's vision. Tampa's "window frame of opportunity," allowed them to view the strategic or (why concrete issues), and the tactical or (how remedial actions). Increasing Tampa Police Department's effectiveness on the strategic issues required changing the way that they did the business of policing.

The Department's vision, mission statement, goals and objectives, had absolute clarity. This police agency reduced criminal offenses by 56 percent. The Department's officers began to realize their potential and recognize the future opportunities.

CONCLUSION

Telling the story from a personal point of view provides leadership direction. This form of storytelling describes the star performer's point of view, the social history, and future destination.

The leader's personal story supports the Problem-Solving Corner: Telling the Story. Storytelling frames the strategic POP problem and connects the problem-solving process. Overlapping story telling qualities provide guidance for developing strategic goals and objectives.

The coordination of strategic planning and patrol operations is essential to successful crime reduction initiatives. The Tampa Police Department is an example of how strategic leadership and planning can make a real difference. The reduction of crime and improvement in quality of life issues for Tampa citizens demonstrates excellent policing efforts.

CHAPTER 3
POSITIVE POLICE LEADERSHIP: FINDING THE PATHWAY

"Management has not given much consideration to the possibility of realizing a higher return on the enormous investment in rank-and-file officers by making fuller use of their knowledge, talents, and skills."
— Herman Goldstein

Police officers staying the daily course are hardworking, disciplined, and dependable. This commitment requires year-after-year service and relentless performance. Professional commitment merits the respect of leaders and the public. Officers committed to policing handle the inevitable pressures that accompany dealing with citizens and crime. They deserve excellent and positive leadership.

When positive police leaders demonstrate selfless service, trustworthiness, and professional expertise, POP policing is enhanced. Subsequently, positive police leadership charisma unfolds as a powerful force multiplier. Positive police leaders have the moral authority to lead and motivate their officers, because they are competent and understand their strengths.

CHAPTER FOCUS

The purpose of this chapter is to highlight positive, problem-oriented leadership. Positive police leadership inspires officers to achieve their special police calling. Trust is the primary factor when influencing officers on the road to superior performance. Positive police leaders influence their officers and build relationships, which eventually unfold the successful execution of the police mission.

OVERVIEW: POSITIVE POLICE LEADERSHIP

Positive leadership is accomplished through consistent and persistent social interaction, which demonstrates character, integrity, and trustworthiness. Officers feel compelled to follow and perform when leaders replicate the correct behaviors. The police

43

commander, leader, or supervisor, who enhances officer interaction, will eventually lead them to the correct pathway.

Failure can be overcome by appealing to the minds and values
of police officers. This is accomplished through positive police
leadership that taps into the officers' character and winning
spirit. The leadership legacy must include: (1) respect and (2)
dignity of officers, civilians, and citizens. Leaders must identify
what they believe and what they stand for, helping officers find
the same through the problem-solving process.

POLICE STAR LEADERSHIP PERFORMERS

Police star performers apply their strengths, identify weaknesses, and seek excellence. Their emotional intelligence paves
the pathway as a catalyst for positive police change. Emotional
intelligence serves as the foundation for positive police leadership
attributes.

Goleman comments, "These are the qualities that mark
people who excel in real life, whose intimate relationships
flourish, who are stars in the workplace. These are also the hall-
marks of character and self-discipline. Of altruism and compassion—basic capacities needed if our society is to thrive."

Interestingly, according to Goleman, "Here the argument for
the importance of emotional intelligence hinges on the link
between sentiment, character, and moral instincts. There is
growing evidence that fundamental ethical stances in life stem
from underlying emotional capacities. For one, impulse is the
medium of emotion; the seed of all impulse is a feeling bursting
to express itself in action ...

Those who are at the mercy of impulse, who lack self-control,
suffer a moral deficiency: The ability to control impulse is the
base of will and character. By the same token, the root of altruism lies in empathy, the ability to read emotions in others;
lacking a sense of another's need or despair, there is no caring.
And if there are any two moral stances that our times call for,
they are precisely these, self-restraint and compassion."

PROFESSIONAL CALLING

Positive leadership inspires others to achieve their special
police calling. Police values are an essential part of living up to

influencing trust. Trust is the primary factor in influencing officers to superior performance. Professional police leaders provide direction, improve the social climate, and provide the means for feedback. Earning trust means keeping promises and commitments, even when it is most difficult.

Diligent police leadership instills the desire to contribute to the effectiveness of the mission. Then, police officers will bring their sense of professionalism, character, and talents to bear on the problem-solving process. Everything is possible when officers recognize their special calling.

Inspirational leadership encourages police officers to embrace an optimistic work ethic. This kind of leader paints a strategic picture, and everyone feels included in the portrait. Sketching graphically requires portraying what success will look like for officers and civilians. Proactive police leaders describe what success feels like, and they are passionate about achieving constructive POP outcomes.

If there ever was a golden rule for successful positive police leadership, it would certainly be: "Do unto others as you would have others do unto you." This straightforward guidepost for police leadership offers great wisdom for gaining police officer cooperation. Moreover, role modeling the correct behavior reaps positive outcomes for police officers, citizens, and the community.

Star performer leadership provides a bridge to influencing officer cooperation and team cohesion. Police leaders give cooperation and, in return, receive officer cooperation. Positive cooperation represents a mutual and interpersonal connection. Positive mutual understanding creates a sense of belonging, pride, and loyalty to the department. Everyone in the department is involved: cooperating and coordinating POP objectives.

Warren Bennis, in his exceptional work, *The Challenges of Leadership in the Modern World*, writes: "The field of leadership studies should attend to how we can develop leaders who understand relationships and communication, who can manage themselves and others with wisdom, creativity, and values." The following chapter addresses that positive leadership style and professional attributes.

LEADERSHIP AND VALUES

Every police leader requires values and ethical standards that provide the pathway for officers to follow. Values also provide the guidance for police officers to anticipate professional direction. Positive policing requires considerable reflection regarding values, and police ethical requirements that support quality service. Police leaders support superior police standards when they role model excellent character behaviors. They encourage police officer progress in their efforts to provide quality service.

Character serves as the foundation for trust; however, without expertise and competence, complete trust is not possible. When police officers confront a critical incident situation where lives are at stake, competency remains the first priority. Excellent leadership is by example, and demonstrates trustworthiness through character, and competent behaviors. Police officers need excellent role models to follow. The balancing act of professional policing, confronting crisis events, and family life, remains a constant struggle.

Ethics represent the guidance or rules for professional police behavior. Police organizational goals work best when they are analogous with the officer's personal values and ethics. Integrity concerns character and moral courage. Officers acknowledging and adhering to their beliefs, offer excellent police service. Police officers who have these personal qualities are trusted and empowered.

Police leaders are the standard-bearers for professional behavior. Teaching values, team thinking, commitment, and quality police service requires consistent and persistent effort. The police value system focuses on honesty and candor: essential ingredients for mission achievement. Values serve as filters for unethical behavior and focus the light of truth in the darkness.

Values serve as a compass and roadmap that sustain one's journey to finding the correct direction. Professional ethics plot a higher road that requires truth and genuine self-exploration. Refer to Figure 3-1 to review steps for carrying the banner for police Values, Ethics, and Integrity.

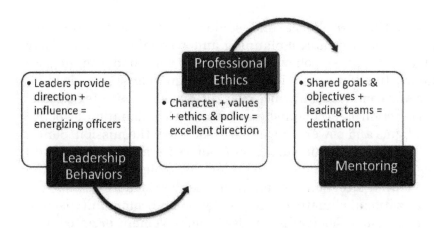

Figure 3-1. Values, Ethics, and Integrity

Truthfulness and kept promises indicate character; however, keeping a pledge can be difficult if honesty and conviction are penalized. Telling the truth and keeping promises are essential attributes when communicating and developing relationships with police officers. Leaders with reputations for competency, truth, and integrity motivate officers to follow and comply, because the latter have faith in the leadership. Respect and support for leaders who demonstrate their trustworthiness instills confidence in officers.

Professional officers apply internalized values and ethics to everyday law enforcement duties. Advocating an ethical climate is the easy part of leadership; the strength to dissuade temptation can be difficult. Leadership requires that commanders encourage integrity, values, and specific police ethical behaviors.

Positive police leaders who demonstrate character build a reputation for reliability and credibility. Leaders who fulfill promises and demonstrate moral courage build fellowship. Excellent leaders stand for what is just, place duty and honor first, and accept responsibility when they are wrong. Positive police leadership demands trustworthiness and emotional intelligence.

LEADERSHIP COORDINATION

The Chief of Police and senior leaders retain exclusive authority over strategic planning and systemic decisions. They provide guidance, policy, and direction for middle managers/ leaders. In addition, senior leaders (commanders) provide guidance and command influence over the vision and strategic goals.

Direction is accomplished through a combination of police paradigms and power sharing, to accomplish the mission. Senior leaders assess middle managers /leaders for abilities and readiness to perform the mission. This level of leadership provides the vision and direction. In addition, senior leaders assess the organizational climate, crime problems, and community issues.

The senior leadership style is achievement-oriented and establishes high expectations of excellence. Moreover, at this level, leadership requires allowing middle managers/leaders to achieve POP goals and objectives. Senior leaders are more likely to clarify goals, expectations, and allow middle managers/leaders to set performance objectives.

Middle managers/leaders earn officer trust when they demonstrate worthiness and articulate accurate mission requirements. Excellent middle leadership requires: (1) character and (2) competency. Middle managers/leaders typically earn officer respect when they are POP and tactically proficient. In addition, respect is gained when middle managers make sound decisions during critical incidents events.

The middle managers/leaders empowerment of officers and staff sets the foundation for Intelligence-Led Policing (ILP). Lieutenants (shift or platoon commanders) follow guidance provided by middle managers/leaders. Middle managers/leaders are essential in the process of influencing officers to pursue POP goals and objectives. They have the power and authority to encourage officers and reward their efforts. At this level, middle leaders have a great deal of authority and a significant amount of power.

Positive leadership requires the management of both formal and informal power. Formal power constitutes the leader's official rank and position. Informal power is less obvious; police officers confer this power because of the leader's qualities. Excellent leadership focuses on the informal power base, thereby doubling the leader's advantage by gaining officer support for formal operations. Refer to Figure 3-2 for an illustration of Formal and Informal Power bases.

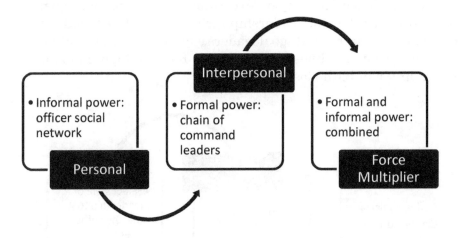

Figure: 3-2. Formal and Informal Power Bases

Middle managers/leaders, captains, and lieutenants, are "gatekeepers" who control resources. The officers and supervisors (sergeants and corporals) cannot perform without the necessary equipment, logistical resources, and personnel reinforcement. Middle managers focus on support, action, and results in the POP programming efforts. They make sure that the team effort is recognized, and every member gets credit for success. Give credit where and when it is due, and to those who deserve it.

Moreover, middle managers understand the appropriate use of conceptual and human relations skills. Communication and human relations skills are of paramount importance. Superior conceptual planning skills mean little without officer support. Regardless of how well-calculated the plan, failure results without sergeant and officer participation.

PATH-GOAL LEADERSHIP

The positive leadership style that strives for what to do, when to do it, and how to do it, is generally the province of sergeants. Even the directive style of leadership requires guidance, some human relations, and excellent supervision. Sergeants emphasize human relations and technical skills.

More often, the essential element, according to Dick Richards, calls for "Convincing Minds and Winning Hearts," regardless of position or leadership style. According to Vroom, path-goal leadership matches the leadership style with the basic traits of subordinate officers. Path-goal leaders examine the combination of the situation, readiness, and mission. Refer to Figure 3-3 for a description of Path-Goal Leadership.

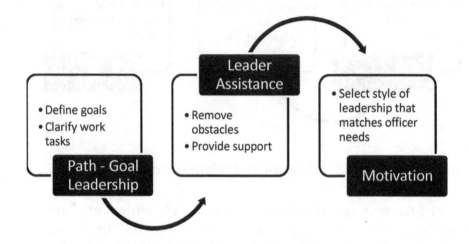

Figure: 3-3. Path-Goal Leadership

Once situational factors fall into place, positive leaders apply the proper leadership style. The path-goal leadership styles are: (1) directive, (2) supportive, and (3) achievement-oriented or participative. The positive leader clarifies goals for subordinate officers, and provides the correct pathway to follow based on individual abilities. Sergeants are likely to apply the directive style of leadership that requires setting performance standards, rules, and related tasks. Positive leadership addresses officer and civilian needs, well-being, and rapport.

LEADERSHIP: THE PATHWAY

Every responsible leader provides a path for others to follow. The Chief of Police, senior leaders, and middle managers, are ultimately responsible, and therefore reluctant to share their power and control. Police lieutenants and sergeants also have accountability and command responsibility requirements. Police leaders may prefer a top-down model of power and control (the para-military model). The top-down approach balances the power in favor of senior leaders and middle managers.

Power and influence require self-control, personal restraint, and excellent decision-making. Moreover, power is the capacity to exert influence and exercise control over officers, the situation, and mission. Power and influence has many sources that assist in accomplishing the mission.

Top-down leadership has limited influence and feedback. The strength of this approach is in external discipline, not internal discipline. However, there is a higher way to improved performance. The bottom-up, problem-solving approach offers the necessary feedback from officers. The combination of these approaches achieves maximum output and cooperation.

The problem-solving approach requires a bottom-up model that encourages participation from community stakeholders, lieutenants, sergeants, and police officers. Power and control are released to empower the bottom-level participants, specifically, officers and civilians. This strategy allows greater flexibility and responsibility in the field, and less power and control for top management.

However, bottom-up (officer leadership) is not likely to succeed without top-down support from commanders. Positive leaders affect real change in police organizations when they inspire the minds of police officers. Command leadership provides the direction, support, and logistics to accomplish the mission.

Bottom-up leadership is a hypothetical ideal; the reality on the street is that it conflicts with good practice. Effective leadership comes from the top-down and releases the potential of supervisors and their officers. Police executives must win the support of police officers through effective decision-making strategies, which put into practice the greater good.

Superior top-down leadership empowers those below and gives them the logical impression that their participation is valued. The achievement of any mission requires leadership and discipline from top management. Once this is accomplished, the leadership from the bottom-up unfolds in a natural manner. Then the human potential from police officers is released to merge in a powerful midway equation.

Power is the ability to accomplish what one desires and the capacity to influence officers and civilians. These ideal models can never be absolute. Communication and intelligence resembles a circular cycle. Feedback requires the coordination of top-down and bottom-up styles of management and empowerment. The communication chain starts with lieutenants, sergeants, and officers closest to the problem. They are initially empowered to make decisions within their defined area of responsibility.

The mission requirements and problem-solving process require empowering officers at the line operation level. This demonstrates their importance and value in the decision-making process. However, the achievements of the police agency, mission, and plans are accomplished through focus, discipline, and support power from senior leaders.

Problem-solving officers support their leaders and team while in the midst of challenge and controversy. They are loyal followers and base their bond on trust. Their focus on loyalty and command guidance is important. First-line supervisors and their officers pursue information in the Operations Order to identify their problem-solving destination. The operations order and coaching teams help commanders accomplish POP mission requirements. The essential factor: flexibility for successful implementation at the execution level.

PROBLEM-SOLVING CORNER: OPERATIONS ORDER

The Operations Order (OPORD) is the primary order that is given for a mission; however, it is not the only type of order that may be issued. A Warning Order, or WARNO, is given in advance of the OPORD to let officers under the command know that they may be receiving an Operations Order. The WARNO contains a few basic details of the situation and what the mission may entail. However, much of the pertinent information for a proper Operations Order is still forthcoming.

Once an OPORD is given, the situation may change before the mission is actually begun. Also, during the operation, the situation may change so that the Operations Order must be modified. In these cases, the commander will issue a Fragmentary Order, or a FRAGO. The FRAGO will state exactly how the situation and /or mission changed and what must be done to make up for the change.

Situation

- Community problem
- Police operations
- Partners
- Attachments and detachments

Mission: **Defined by the problem**

Execution

- Patrol operations
- Intelligence-led policing
- Criminal information
- Intelligence analysis
- Crime analysis

Unit/patrol Tasking

- Traffic control
- Fire services support
- Emergency rescue
- Coordinating instructions
    1. Time or condition when a plan or order becomes effective
    2. Commanders critical information
    3. Risk reduction control measures
    4. Rules of engagement
    5. Force protection

Sustainment/logistics

- Support concept
- Material and service support
- Personnel
- Hospital/medical support
- Military support
- As required

Command and Control

- Command
- Control
- Staff support
- Communication equipment

Source: The information contained above is adapted from United States Army Field Manual 101-5, Staff Organization and Operations, 31 May 1997

PARTICIPATORY MANAGEMENT

Problem-solving power sharing involves participatory management. There are three foremost POP empowerment strategies: (1) participatory management, (2) team leadership, and (3) the exception/delegation principle. Delegation of authority gives greater freedom to officers to act appropriately and respond in a timely manner.

The individual officer or group of officers has realistic input before a course of action is implemented. This is not always easy and it is time-consuming; however, it serves as a driving force for acceptance and participation. More importantly, it inspires officers to excellence and prepares them to accept change.

Positive leadership allows officers and civilians to manage themselves. Empowerment stimulates imagination, creativity, and increased output of policing effort. The leader gets out of the way, providing guidance and direction if needed.

When police leaders share power, officers allocate power, and ultimately it returns to leaders in the form of superior performance. Empowering officers does not mean relinquishing control; it requires establishing appropriate boundaries. The concept of control may appear as a contradiction to empowerment; however, control is essential to positive outcomes.

THE EXCEPTION PRINCIPLE

The "Exception Principle" is a fundamental element in effective positive police leadership. Specific exceptions to problem-solving procedures may arise that require leadership flexibility. Significant departure from methods of operation or police policy requires leadership approval. Police officers need to have an understanding of this principle to appreciate leader accountability.

There are many advantages to delegation of authority and the "Exception Principle." Delegation unburdens leaders from minute details of daily police operations. Most importantly, delegation encourages team members to perform their part of the mission. Police leader time and attention can be devoted to major goals and objectives rather than specific tasks.

Police leaders are accountable for accomplishing the mission through their officers. Empowering officers through effective delegation is an excellent leadership method for increasing productivity and service to the community. Police managers transfer authority, not responsibility, to accomplish goals and objectives.

The explanation of tasks, conditions, and standards transpires before delegation of authority. The process of empowering officers creates accountability for their actions. Officers take responsibility for properly executing mission orders. Accountability of performance means reacting in a timely manner and assuming responsibility for behaviors. Refer to Figure 3-4 for an analysis and example of the Delegation Process.

Figure 3-4. Delegation Process

The delegation process can lead to better decision-making, because it permits officers who are closer to the POP problem-solving process to use their own judgment. Police leaders are occasionally reluctant to delegate, because they fear officer mistakes and reprimands from command. Mistakes can be made by anyone in the chain of command; however, adequate controls and feedback can prevent worst case scenarios. Anticipate police officer mistakes that represent normal components of the learning process. Police leaders cannot perform every task. Appropriate leadership delegation offers opportunities for fewer mistakes due to leader burnout.

TEAM LEADERSHIP

Police leaders provide initiatives and serve as role models for problem-solving. They show respect for everyone in the police organization, as well as police team members. In return, police leaders gain respect for giving respect. Team leaders earn respect through cooperation and providing opportunities for participation. Positive police leaders permit officers to participate in formulating the ground rules and decision- making. Furthermore, participation improves cooperation, enthusiasm, and a "team compliance" attitude. Officers claim ownership, and enhance the leader's team position and personal power.

Teamwork requires relying on interdependency to accomplish the mission. However, there is the need to know, understand, and trust team members. This kind of relationship takes time to build. Officers share a common relationship and contribute to a collective commitment to the POP team.

Moreover, strategies that create competent teams require effort and positive police leadership. Several advantages unfold when leaders are supportive and cooperate with officers: respect and cooperation at a higher level of performance. Officers work together as team, demonstrating high morale, and direction from police leaders. POP team efforts produce: (1) initiative, (2) ingenuity, and (3) enthusiasm.

Additional cooperation benefits include: (1) feeling part of team that cares about officer opinions, (2) officers feel like they serve as a member on a supportive department and team, (3) participation identifies talented officers, and (4) officers develop a sense of pride and importance.

Team building requires a self-governing, positive police leadership style, which provides the means for informal leadership to emerge. POP teams play a vital role in the direction and work allocation that support the police mission. POP team members build group loyalty and trust one another.

FOCUS POINTS

Police leaders, who understand the strategic picture and how department goals and objectives are related, encourage direction. The superior leader defines the strategic picture to accomplish a sense of purpose. In brief, share the vision, instill the objectives, and achieve feedback. Most importantly, recognize individual officer performance and celebrate a team's successful accomplishments.

Commanders set the climate for change and problem-solving. In essence, it is not top-down (senior leaders) or bottom-up (officers); the best way combines both approaches. Power to command is not always the result of official position or authority. One can apply force or control from an informal position, influencing officers in an informal or personal manner.

POP leadership represents a positive leadership system that requires excellent character. Understanding the differences between right and wrong describes the influence of values. Police leadership values influence behaviors and determine if police officers will decide to follow their leader's guidance.

Excellent leadership prepares for responsibility, and cares about the welfare of police officers. Treating officers as responsible contributors transcends power into superior and trusting relationships. Positive police leaders identify priorities and follow-up procedures. Praise officers who helped achieve the mission, goals, and objectives.

Positive leaders strive for approval and respect. The most important attribute an effective leader can demonstrate: character. A police leader with character has the ability to discern right and wrong. Effective leaders keep their word and promises. Doing so encourages officer trust and respect. Positive police leaders who tell the truth: earn officer respect.

Positive police leaders are good listeners. They encourage feedback and act on good information. Dedicated police leaders assist their officers and develop and support their efforts. Positive police leaders expect cooperation and teamwork; then they return it to their officers and POP police teams.

CONCLUSION

Senior leaders are strongly committed to conceptual thinking. Human relations are always a consideration and connected to "convincing minds and winning the officers' morale." Feedback from the bottom-up (officers and sergeants) and top down (senior leaders, and middle leaders) ensures superior solutions. Using power wisely remains essential to building leadership pathways and positive police leadership influence.

PART II
POSITIVE COMMUNICATION PATHWAYS

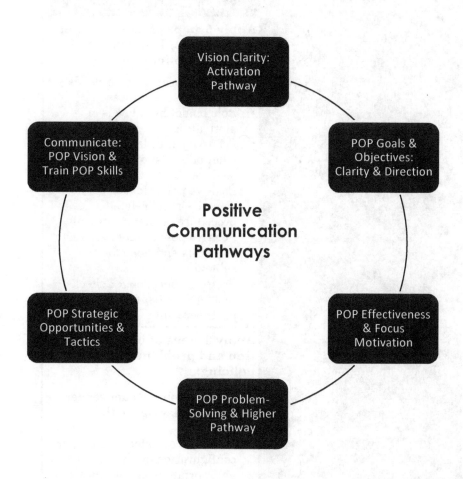

THE POSITIVE LEADERSHIP FOUNDATIONS AND GUIDEPOST

Leadership Foundations	Guidepost Behaviors
• Motivational leadership • Positive Police Leadership and Emotional Intelligence (EQ) Skills • Building rapport • Police excellence • Defining goals & objectives • Finding the higher pathway • Path-goal leadership • Motivation: thread of leadership • Leadership removes obstacles • Align positive outcomes • Celebrates accomplishments	**Apply 6 steps of motivational leadership & Problem-Oriented Policing:** • Assess officer or team needs and level of readiness • Role model high levels of motivation • Positive police leader defines what officer(s) or team need to achieve • Positive police leader sets objectives and related procedures to achieve results • Positive police leader shares EQ skills and hope for achieving objectives • Positive police leader checks task accomplishment and praises results
• Positive leader/communication • Communication mode • Channels of communication • Manner and technique • Staff briefings • Achieving message clarity • CAPRA Model • Communication feedback	**Apply 3 steps of communication and problem-oriented policing:** • Positive police leader sender • Positive message to the receiver • Messages encoded into proper configuration or channel that is appropriate to communicating meaning or ideas
• Positive POP police training • Building the EQ training climate • Problem-solving training • Diverse training cycles • Adapting learning models • Cascading training down • Training bubbling Up • Community training	• Positive policing teaching cycles allow special POP operating teams to implement new elements and modify operations • Instructional/learning is recycled back up chain of command from operating teams • Teams continuously customize behaviors and tactics based on field experiences

CHAPTER 4
POSITIVE MOTIVATIONAL LEADERSHIP: FINDING THE WAY

"Boredom and lack of challenge are associated with many aspects of policing. Charging officers with the responsibility to work substantive problems—to use their time, talent, and imagination in doing so—will make their job more stimulating."

— Herman Goldstein

Police officers represent valuable assets in police organizations. Motivating police officers is the most significant challenge of the problem-solving philosophy. The POP approach requires motivating and getting the work done through police officers. Police leaders guide officers toward the accomplishment of POP goals and objectives, thus accomplishing the mission.

Positive leaders provide greater attention to officers and motivate their desire to succeed. Some police officers discover the light of professionalism and commitment, while others require external incentives and explanation. Officers who display high energy and enthusiasm will eventually find greater satisfaction in POP policing.

CHAPTER FOCUS

The purpose of this chapter is to describe the leadership motivation process. Finding the way requires understanding POP leadership requirements and motivation principles. Furthermore, this chapter content elaborates on achieving direction, sustaining police professional motivation and achieving pinnacle priorities.

OVERVIEW: MOTIVATION

Positive police leaders create a motivational climate that delivers high performance officers. Understanding the principles of motivation encourages police officer achievement. Motivation may be defined as: internal and external forces that drive individuals, teams, and POP policing accomplishments.

Motivational potential originates from within each officer. The leadership challenge is to shape the officer's motivation to

conform to the department's goals and objectives. Positive police
leaders place emphasis on creating enthusiasm and focusing on
identified objectives. Star performer leadership opens the door to
superior motivation by setting clear objectives and providing
opportunities for success.

The First Step: Conduct a preliminary examination of individual officer and POP team member skills. Police leaders
examine abilities, talents, and experience factors that facilitate
successful performance levels. The POP training level is the most
significant factor in expertise assessment. If training and
expertise levels are not sufficient, achievement and performance
require further training.

Positive police leaders provide the goals, objectives, and
pathways for their officers' professional effort.

The Second Step: Provide resources and project-specific
logistics.

The Third Step: Step out-of-the-way and permit officers to
perform without unnecessary restrictions.

Some of the strongest motivational incentives include: (1) the
feeling of personal officer achievement, (2) the respect officers
gain from being part of an excellent team and department, (3)
performing the POP mission goals and objectives in a superior
manner, and (4) the pride of being part of the police professional
team effort.

POLICE STAR LEADERSHIP PERFORMERS

The first leadership requirement for building a productive
police climate: learn the principles of emotional intelligence (EQ)
and motivation. Police star performers understand the basics of
motivational theory that are necessary to encourage and inspire
their officers and POP teams. The first imperative: emotional intelligence and motivation require the ability to read people.

The next motivation imperative: touch the heart to gain
influence and understand the needs of officers. Stephen Covey's
Fifth Habit and next imperative sums it up: "seek first to understand, before you are understood."

**The following basic four steps describe the role of posi-
tive police leadership and motivation.**

The First Step: Police star performer leaders demonstrate and role model high levels of motivation for officers to follow. Leadership influence means demonstrating trustworthiness and personal character, attributes that encourage officers to follow. Understanding the problems that police officers and teams stumble upon when implementing POP objectives represents an additional starting point.

The Second Step: Motivation requires that positive police leaders understand what teams need to achieve.

The Third Step: Establish POP objectives and define the related procedures to achieve them. Then, define the particular time frame and window of opportunity for the accomplishment of those POP objectives.

The Fourth Step: Police star performer leaders share hope for successfully achieving the POP objectives and positive outcomes. Increasing officer motivation means visualizing what it will be like for them to achieve mission requirements. The essence of motivation: police leaders must influence officers and focus on the future.

MOTIVATION: THE HIGHER PATHWAY

The higher pathway requires allowing officers to arrive at self-enlightenment. Leaders define how officer needs and goals coincide with those of the police organization. Motivation is not simply about pain or pleasure outcomes for the officer. Once police officers understand the higher goals of selfless service to the community, they are more likely to follow that noble cause.

Cause and effect relationships can influence officer performance. Positive police leaders determine what officers want, then seek ways to link those needs to organization goals and objectives. Meaningful incentives and rewards can establish the officers' connection to favorable police administration outcomes. Generally, the police department will reap desired results when officers perceive their desired results or rewards are connected to police goals and objectives. Refer to Figure 4-1 for an illustration of Encouraging Motivation.

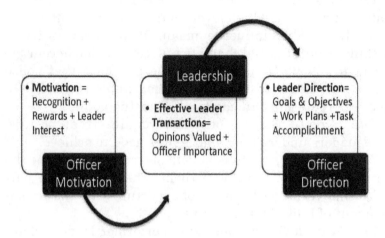

Figure 4-1. Encouraging Motivation

Positive police leaders realize that problem-solving requires successful actions with, by, and through police officers. Effective leaders pay attention to officer needs and desires. Police star performers understand the necessity to create a work environment that offers recognition, team achievement, and fulfillment.

BUILDING POLICING BRIDGES

Positive police leaders understand that police officers represent an essential component of the leadership equation. Police chiefs, middle managers/leaders, and sergeants also focus on strategic goals and objectives. The results represent officer and department employee efforts and achievements. POP accomplishments deserve appropriate praise and recognition.

Officer-oriented police leaders are concerned with understanding officer behaviors. Effective police leadership requires predicting, with some degree of accuracy, how officers will react to given situations. Why do officers behave one way at one time, and in a very different manner at other times? The forces that cause officers to act define the word: "motivation."

The motivational process builds its foundation in goal-directed behaviors, which are encouraged toward satisfying a need or desire. Some needs are universal, while others arise from the officers' surroundings or environment. Additional needs relate to officers in general and some solely to individual officers.

Officers are motivated when they have a need. However, what happens if an officer has two simultaneous needs? Once an officer meets one need, then they would then be motivated to act in some way that would satisfy another need. In general, basic physiological survival needs take precedence over other higher needs. Moreover, increasing police officer participation requires appealing to their understanding and enthusiasm. Then, officers will volunteer their special and individual talents.

IDENTIFYING MOTIVATIONAL NEEDS

Dr. Abraham Maslow arranged a motivational hierarchy of needs, starting with our most basic (or physiological) needs and ranging upward to include our needs for self-fulfillment or actualization and transcendence. While each officer is an individual, and needs to be treated as an individual, certain overlapping needs exist. Refer to Figure 4-2 and examine examples of police agency, leader, and officer overlapping Maslow's Hierarchy of Needs.

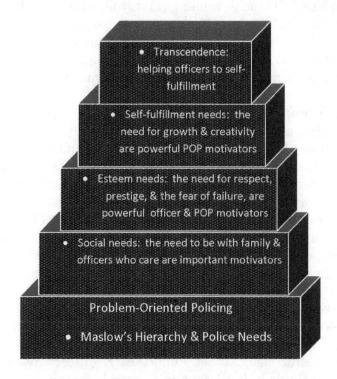

Figure 4-2. Maslow's Hierarchy of Needs

Transcendence: The need to help others self-actualize or reach self-fulfillment. Arrival at this level requires understanding positive police leadership and possessing emotional intelligence.

Self-fulfillment or Actualization: (1) personal growth and (2) self-fulfillment. These needs are related to: achieving important goals, expressing creative ideas, and developing for oneself an important place in a community, nation, or the world. An officer has the desire to make use of their human capacities, to grow, and reach their full potential. The need for self-actualization and transcendence are positive police leadership requirements, and require the development of emotional intelligence.

Aesthetic Needs: (1) beauty, (2) balance and (3) form. Aesthetic needs may overlap some higher level needs.

Cognitive Needs: (1) gaining knowledge, (2) meaning, and (3) self-awareness. Education and police training attempt to meet these needs. Growth and development are import to the application of positive policing and emotional intelligence.

Esteem Needs: (1) achievement, (2) status, (3) responsibility, and (4) reputation. The need for respect, prestige, status, and power over others is important. The need to avoid feelings of failure or inferiority, and to protect one's ego, is a related need. Ego needs have the most common connection to motivating police officers.

Belongingness and Love Needs: (1) family, (2) affection, (3) relationships, and (4) work group relationships. Officers need to be with other people, and have others understand them. The need for help from others, moreover, the need for affection from others, is important. Social needs can serve as a positive motivator for promoting POP objectives.

Safety Needs: (1) protection, (2) security, (3) order, (4) limits and (5) stability. The need for security is an important primary level function. Officers need to seek a safe, stable environment, and to obtain items they need for survival and security. The connection for meeting POP objectives is remote when the safety needs have the first priority.

Physiological and Biological Needs: (1) air, (2) water, (3) food, and (4) human physical relationships. Everyone has the need for rest and sleep. Most importantly, officers need to maintain body fluids in balance, and to keep body temperature at an optimal level to ensure survival. Certainly, the physiological needs have the first priority for human continued existence. The basic life needs: (1) air, (2) food, (3) water, (4) shelter, (5) warmth, (6) sex, and (7) sleep.

The dividing lines between these levels of needs are not precise. The classifications and the needs contained within overlap. As officers experience need satisfaction, they are more likely to find a higher order of needs; however, the basic need requirements remain. As a result, the following needs most likely motivate officers: esteem, self-actualization, and transcendence levels of Maslow's Needs hierarchy.

Self-fulfillment or actualization, and transcendence needs, can serve as important positive police leadership motivators. Police officers operating at that level perform well, the result of inner motivation. Police officers have the potential to achieve this level. However, police officer social needs are important motivational factors in POP problem-solving.

The exception to this principle: officers in critical incident or life-threatening situations. When an officer is driven by more than one motive, they may present conflict or not be compatible. One need might require more support or opposes the satisfaction of another. When the officer finds they can attain one need only at the expense of another, frustration can result.

Positive police leaders are at their best when they are motivating, training, and helping officers. Effective police leaders and sergeants must remain officer and citizen-centered. Police leaders receive two types of compensation: (1) mission accomplishment and (2) the satisfaction that comes from leading and motivating police officers. Their highest accomplishment: help police officers achieve their full potential and professional calling.

Police star performer leaders make an effort to determine the wants and needs of each officer and address their right to be treated as an individual. They must attempt to accomplish officer connections. However, positive police leaders require that the emphasis be on: "We as a team and department" rather than the "I" or individual approach.

MOTIVATION AND PERFORMANCE

Frederick Herzberg's research provides unique insight and observations about motivating officers. His research findings suggest that things that dissatisfy employees (officers and civilians) are entirely different from those that satisfy them. The factors or relationships that lead to dissatisfiers or satisfiers are distinctly different. Refer to Figures 4-3-A and 4-3-B for the author's adaptation of a graphic illustration of Herzberg's Motivators and Research factors.

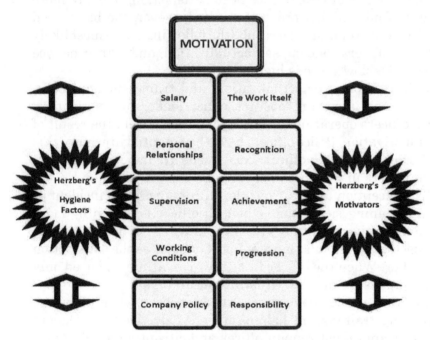

Figure 4-3-A. Herzberg's Motivators

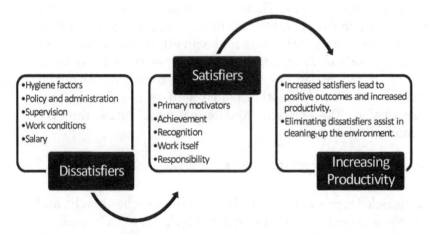

Figure 4-3-B. Herzberg's Research

The important thing for police leaders to remember is that the elimination of dissatisfaction does not automatically provide satisfaction for the officer(s). Police leaders who eliminate dissatisfaction for officers or civilians should not assume that they have created satisfaction. They have only eliminated that dissatisfaction. The primary motivators for job satisfaction are achievement and recognition. The second and third motivators include: (1) how the officer or civilian employee views the work itself and (2) sense of responsibility.

According to Herzberg research, when leaders eliminate that which dissatisfies, leaders are merely cleaning up the environment. The leaders have not created satisfaction or a motivator. The elimination of dissatisfaction is merely an improvement in organizational hygiene factors.

Herzberg's research labeled satisfiers as motivators because those factors had a positive effect on increasing the officers' motivation, effort, and output. Officers and civilians are not motivated by failure; they are motivated by achievement, according to his research.

Achievement and recognition represent the strongest motivators; police leaders who want officers to participate in the problem-solving process apply the following:

- Leave the office and spend time in the field talking to officers doing the work.
- Recognize the work effort of officers as soon as you have the knowledge of the merits of their efforts.
- Keep a record of the achievement and list ways that police leader can credit the achievement.
- Do not neglect the small wins; they are important to the officer.

The code words for incentive to perform will always remain a police officer's basic need for recognition and achievement. "Thank you," "Excellent contribution to the mission," and "Your performance was outstanding" all represent watch words for police leadership.

MANAGERS AND MOTIVATION

Robert R. Blake and Jane S. Mouton's research on the Managerial Grid of management practices revealed interesting results concerning motivation. Their Managerial Grid identifies various kinds of managerial behaviors. The grid's vertical axis represents concern for people; the horizontal axis, concern for production.

A study of grid manager behaviors provides readers with a system to describe their own managerial style and those of others. Moreover, it describes organization leaders as a whole, as well as a framework of ideas for increasing the effectiveness of managerial practices and attitudes.

The Managerial Grid is an excellent example of leadership for production and concern for people. Furthermore, it can serve as an assessment model for police agencies dealing with changing climate circumstances. Police managers may prefer one leadership style or organizational climate; however, emergency circumstances can change and disrupt the climate. Police leaders require flexibility rather than fixed organizational responses or leadership styles.

For most organizations, Blake and Mouton recommend: top right-corner (Team Management) showing high concern for officers, attaining performance by integrating officers and tasks. The upper left-hand corner describes (Country Club Management): placing the level of social contentment before performance. The lower left-hand corner describes (Impoverished Management): having little concern for officers or performance. The lower right corner describes (Task Management): out-put and performance priority, driving officers to complete the basic tasks. Refer to Figure 4-4 for an illustration of their Managerial Grid.

Team Management and Task Management serve as POP policing ideal managerial combinations. Country Club Management does not serve POP policing goals and objectives well. Impoverished Management is the worst managerial approach. In fact, the Country Club Management and Impoverished Management neglect the welfare of the community and endanger police officer lives.

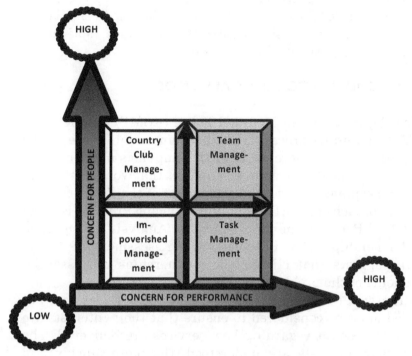

Figure 4-4. The Managerial Grid

FINDING THE PATHWAY

Positive leader pathways unleash officer and community potential and creativity. Excellent police leaders take the high road, encouraging motivation and community development. The CAPRA Model represents a creative force that influences the momentum to encourage positive motivational factors. Convincing officers that they can make a difference will help them find the pathway and encourage others to seek the high road.

The CAPRA Model envisions the direction and provides motivation for a higher pathway to policing and community accomplishment. The CAPRA Model is a proven method for explaining a strategic point of view and providing direction. Most importantly, CAPRA provides the strategic frame of reference for motivating police officers, citizens, clients, and partners.

For example, the police department focuses on the motivational pathway and important issues. Police goals that align practice with the mission, clients, partnerships, and citizens, represent core motivational focus points. Refer to the Royal Canadian Mounted Police (RCMP) Problem-Solving Corner below for an example of a vision model that provides motivation, direction, and a pathway for officers to follow.

PROBLEM-SOLVING CORNER: CAPRA MODEL

The Royal Canadian Mounted Police (RCMP) complements the SARA planning process with the human enterprise of the POP process. The difference is in the emphasis of clients and partnerships. The RCMP approach realizes that working through and with people is an essential component of the POP process.

The approach of RCMP Community Policing Problem-Solving Model, **CAPRA** (C = Clients, A = Acquire/Analysis Information, P = Partnerships, R = Response, A = Assessment of Action taken), suggests that clients and partnerships are essential components of the problem-solving process.

Clients: All who have an interest in the services that are provided must be considered to ensure that their interests are taken into account regarding how services are delivered. The better their interests are understood, the more quickly and effectively their needs can be met, as well as their demands and expectations in terms of service delivery (defining problems, establishing priorities, deployment of personnel, and assessing how service standards are met).

Client understanding improves and helps to dissipate potentially violent situations before they erupt. Having this understanding helps mobilize the community to assist in achieving safe homes and safe streets by solving community problems, and generates workable and sustainable preventive actions.

Two types of clients are identified: (1) Direct clients are those with whom an agency interacts at various points in service delivery or investigations; (2) Indirect clients are those not directly involved in an incident, or its investigation, but have an interest in its outcome either because of the way it was handled, or because of the association of the incident to similar incidents.

Direct Clients: People whom police agencies come into contact on a daily basis, in service delivery, or in problem-solving situations, and include individual citizens (victims, witnesses, concerned citizens, suspects, etc.). In addition, concerned citizen groups, internal clients, policy centers, regions, divisions, individual employees, etc., and various agencies and departments are direct clients.

Indirect Clients: Clients might include business communities (where, for example, a series of thefts have occurred); interest groups (e.g., women's groups, where, for example, a sexual assault has occurred); cultural groups (where, for example, discriminatory practices have occurred in the workplace).

RCMP defines **Partnership:** "Developing and maintaining partnerships is the third element of this operational model. Partners are individuals or groups who can assist police agencies in providing quality service. They may be internal or external to the police agency, or your unit within the agency.

Partnerships, like friendships, are established, based on trust. People, who feel that they have been fairly treated in the past, will not hesitate to assist in subsequent endeavors. In the interest of ensuring timely and quality responses, partnerships would be established before there is a problem, and contingency plans should be established to address the most typical kinds of work-related situations that arise. Partnerships should result in mutual benefits.

The RCMP model recognizes that police agencies need to communicate the "message of interdependence" with the community. Police agencies require mutual support systems to improve the delivery of services. This joint effort requires communication, strength of purpose, and trust. Interdependence requires choosing to depend on others to accomplish the police mission successfully.

Acquiring and Analyzing Information: This includes gathering information essential to the investigation, or handling the investigation incident. Many police officers restrict their information gathering to the facts directly related to the specific incident of occurrence. The more comprehensive the information gathered, the better an agency is able to effectively analyze a problem.

Response: Response is about applying strategies to solve community problems. An agency that has done an effective job in the preceding parts of CAPRA can develop appropriate response strategies that have a high probability of success. For every call for assistance or intervention, police have available to them four major types of response strategies: (1) service, (2) protection, (3)

enforcement, and (4) prevention. Service is assisting the public
and referring them to appropriate partners.

Protection is defined as protecting the public, victims, and
those affected by their victimization, in partnership with community agencies and experts. Enforcement entails enforcing laws
through the judicial system so that offenders are held accountable. Finally, prevention involves preventing problems from
occurring or escalating through (1) intervention, (2) proactive
problem-solving, and (3) education.

Remember that there are usually multiple responses from
which to choose. The skill is in choosing the option that results in
the fewest number of negative consequences. There are six
possible solutions to a problem: (1) totally eliminating the problem; (2) substantially reducing the problem; (3) reducing the
harm created by the problem; (4) improving police responses
to the problem; (5) redefining problem responsibilities; and
(6) determining that the perceived problem is really not a problem after all.

Assessment: Assessment is the evaluation of the effectiveness of the response that has been chosen. The determination of
what worked and what did not work is critical, so that modification to the response or complete response changes can be made
if necessary. Ongoing monitoring of a situation is essential to the
continuous improvement and the discussion of present and future
problem-solving efforts. Formalizing the assessment with written
documentation allows for others to learn from your problem-
solving efforts. It should be remembered that other officers are
dealing day in and day out with the same problems; therefore,
there is much that can be learned from others' successes and
failures."

Source: Royal Canadian Mounted Police, Facilitators Guide to the RCMP Learning Maps: CAPRA
Problem Solving Model (Ottawa, Ontario, 1993).

LEADERSHIP MOTIVATION AND COORDINATION

Effective police leaders understand that their primary responsibility is to accomplish the mission through their clients, partners, and officers. In most cases, this means motivating and
working with police officers and civilians, because leaders need
them more than they need leaders. Ultimately, positive police

leaders receive their rewards when officers are motivated to achieve.

Police leaders succeed only when officers and communities experience success. Therefore, leaders need to ensure they use their power wisely in support of their efforts. The basic leadership requirement is to accept full responsibility for the failures as well as the wins of officers. The most positive leadership credit is the acknowledgment of police officers, which bears testimony to the leader's presence and support.

Star performer leadership motivates officers by setting the example and identifying correct problem-solving behaviors. Effective leadership empowers officers, builds confidence, self-esteem, and ultimately competence. Police leaders generate power by sharing power, because their source of power comes from officers and civilians. When releasing power, police leaders can achieve significant goals and objectives.

Effective police leaders can identify solutions to core problems in their communities through the application of the POP paradigm. A comprehensive description of community chronic problems can solicit long-term solutions. Moreover, problem-solving solutions may be achieved through direct participation from citizens and police officers.

Concerned police leaders eliminate obstacles by providing judicious and logistical support. One area that may go unnoticed by police leaders: external influences and obstacles to officer performance. There are support and logistical items necessary to support performance that may be beyond officer control. For example, police managers may not provide proper security clearance for officers. This kind of omission could deny officers the ability to obtain critical criminal information.

FOCUS POINTS

The POP mission requires being aware of the community terrain, and unexpected turns in the pathways. Police leaders need the vision and foresight to change, and encourage teams to follow. Planning and reorganization of police personnel, logistics, and department organization are always important factors.

Creative police leaders improvise imaginative strategies that reinforce motivation and performance. POP problem-solving is challenging and can serve as a motivating influence.

Problem-solving offers opportunities to demonstrate innovative and creative thinking. Positive police leaders encourage POP motivational incentives that can provide opportunities for the community service.

Police service demands increased imagination and creativity because of the competing demands for services.

Establishing and maintaining partnerships increase the amount of resources (i.e., personnel power, finances, etc.) and solutions available for addressing a particular community problem. The more partners and clients the police agency engages, the more trust that is built for increasing effective solutions. The primary goal: POP having an impact and lasting effect to make the community a safe place to live.

Partnerships can include anyone within the organization, other government departments or agencies, or the community who can assist in providing better quality and timely service.

Partners might surface from within a police agency, or externally, from the community (e.g., doctors, social workers, psychologists, scientists, lab technicians, canine specialists, fire fighters, clergy, and colleagues with experience or expertise in a particular area).

Police leaders and officers need inspirational and challenging incentives. Problem-solving encourages police personnel to break with routine patrol procedures and make an individual contribution to the prevention of crime and disorder. Problem-solving creates opportunities for police leaders to interact meaningfully with their officers and encourage motivation.

CONCLUSION

There is no magic antidote for POP performance; the best hope is in police star performer leadership and professional guidance. Excellent performance outcomes demand time and attention in police organizations. Positive leadership and POP can make a significant difference in the community. Officer motivation and POP success requires a conscious effort from police leaders. Police excellence is the result of highly motivated police officers. Motivation and performance is not a quick-fix remedy; it is a tenuous thread of leadership, which requires constant effort.

CHAPTER 5
POSITIVE PROBLEM-SOLVING COMMUNICATION

"Communication between agencies can lead to recognition of common goals, development of mutual respect, and establishment of a working relationship that benefits agencies, the community, and most importantly, the individuals who are subject to some form of control."
— Herman Goldstein

Positive police leaders maximize the benefits of basic methods and forms of communication. Excellent communication skills allow police leaders and their officers to discover pathways to problem-solving. Familiarity with human relations principles opens new avenues for the development of essential police community communication skills. The process is less than perfect and requires constant attention.

Police leaders need to communicate well. When they send accurate and understandable messages without distortion, a positive outcome is likely. Police commanders, leaders, and sergeants, guide officers through careful communication that promotes officer and team potential.

CHAPTER FOCUS

The purpose of this chapter on problem-solving communication is to improve communication feedback in police organizations. Police leaders who demonstrate competence, clarity, and effective communication provide a clear message path for officers to follow. Positive leadership communication provides the pathway for officers and civilians to follow.

OVERVIEW: COMMUNICATION

Communication is defined as the transmission of information from one officer or person to another. However, the common dictionary definition offers an inadequate description. The human communication process is complex and often emotional. Moreover, the ability to understand where the receiver might distort a message is the essence of communication.

The mode, manner, and techniques of the communicator increase receiver understanding and message clarity. The components of the police communication process include: (1) sender, (2) message, and (3) receiver. Communication involves additional, more complex components; it includes understanding the human part of the equation.

Communication is the process of sending accurate messages to police officers, civilian employees, and citizens. The police leader's goal: to produce an intended outcome or change in performance or behavior. Understanding emotional components of communication prevents police communication failure.

The clarity of the communication improves understanding and encourages message acceptance. The end objective of police communication: persuasion. Messages are encoded into proper configurations or channels, appropriate to communicating the meaning or ideas. The term "noise" refers to anything that interferes, disrupts, or inhibits the communication. Refer to Figure 5-1 for an illustration of the basic Components of Communication.

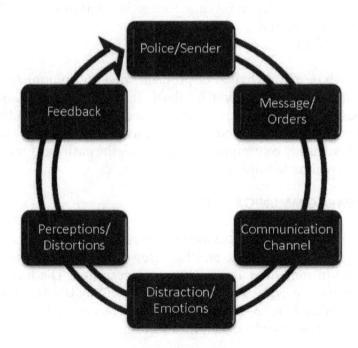

Figure 5-1. Components of Communication

POLICE STAR LEADERSHIP PERFORMERS

Police star leadership performers develop their emotional intelligence (EQ) by listening with an open mind. They send clear and convincing messages, and cultivate open relationships. The positive police leader reads social cues expressed by their officers. These leaders are active listeners and specifically shape their positive speaking content. The flow of information continues until the police leader achieves a positive exchange and mutual understanding concerning the message.

Effective police leaders recognize officer contributions and acknowledge support team efforts. Effective leadership supports a creative, critical thinking, and problem-solving climate that does not protect weaknesses but capitalizes on the collective strengths of police officers. Communication requires the police leader's emotional intelligence competencies and ideal timing.

According to Daniel Goleman's research and book, *Working With Emotional Intelligence*, there are six basic skills of effective communication: (1) active listening skills, (2) asking good follow-up questions, (3) being open-minded, (4) understanding the other person, (5) not interrupting, and (6) asking for suggestions. His research indicated that people prefer working with and relating to others who can successfully communicate their emotions and requests tactfully.

Moreover, positive police leaders have specific communication competencies: (1) Effective police leaders send clear and convincing messages; (2) star performers cultivate empathy with a give-and-take attitude; (3) insightful police leaders cultivate a free flow and exchange of information, until both parties understand each other's viewpoint; and (4) exceptional police leader communication is diplomatic and respectful.

POLICE STRATEGIC COMMUNICATION

Proactive police leadership and problem-solving strategies impact the quality of police services. Significant policing problems can be addressed through guiding principle, communication, and conflict management skills. The call for exceptional police leaders in the field of law enforcement remains a constant requirement for effective police leadership. Superior police leadership requires emotional intelligence and self-control.

Effective police leaders speak and communicate well in advance of their vision, strategy, and tactics. Their communication skills focus on the pathway to vision and goal attainment. Insightful leaders communicate confidence and competence, providing meaningful guidance for others to follow. When positive leaders speak, officers listen and follow their directions.

Police leaders are evaluated not only on what they communicate, but how they express their thoughts, vision, and ideas. They articulate their point of view with clarity and purpose. Police team members are impressed with the content and message delivery.

Police strategic communication seeks to achieve mission clarity, community goals, and objectives. Effective strategic communication requires that internal policing and external community consequences represent end objectives. The strategic picture is about examining opportunities, risks, and correct tactical decisions.

How can one be an effective police leader and communicate well with (1) direct clients, (2) indirect clients, and (3) partners? Positive police leaders encourage strategic communication, providing advice on how to succeed in the community's problem-solving process. Communication goals and objectives include: (1) dealing with community, (2) initiating problem-solving solutions, and (3) preventing and solving crimes.

According to David Bartlett, in his book, *Making Your Point*, strategic communication goals and objectives are addressed before tactical message delivery.

The First Step: Understand what the police leader is trying to accomplish.

The Second Step: Identify with clarity and focus what the message will consist of on a strategic level.

The Third Step: Communicate the point of the message to the intended audience.

Strategic questions may not be examined in the midst of controversy and emotional consequences. Requirements are increasingly stringent in the context of an emergency or crisis situation. Therefore, two persistent questions remain: (1) What are the mission requirements? and (2) What is the police agency trying to communicate? The answers to these two questions address communication management. Refer to Figure 5-2 for an example of Strategic Message Coordination.

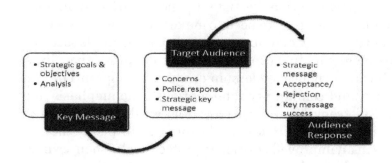

Figure 5-2. Strategic Message Coordination

The first objective of managing issues: define the purpose of the communication. The second objective: establish the framework for debating the issues concerning the target and the strategic outcome. Police agencies seek favorable points of view, including positive outcomes and public opinion. This action demands effective communication and message telling to the intended audience.

Effective police communications require favorable messages and may also be defined as managing the issues. The goal: to achieve a strategic point of view and outcome without communication noise and emotional distortion. Favorable outcomes result from consistent and persistent messages.

For example, community empowerment offers opportunities to focus on crime problems. In addition, empowerment increases the community's sense of competence and self-determination. Communities can overcome learned helplessness when police agencies communicate the correct strategic message.

The message: "fight against crime" implies the notion the police serve as soldiers in a battle. This form of battle communication instills a "we versus them" mentality. The positive message is "we need your support" and without that support, the police cannot prevail alone. The community needs to take responsibility for its part and participate with the police to solve community problems.

Conscientious police leadership advocates a collective sense of responsibility and shared stake in reducing crime. The communication message identifies the concept of social cohesion and community participation. Persistent police positive communication stays on message: "We need to make the community a better place for everyone." Community communication builds social ties that link neighbors in a concerted effort to improve their lives.

Enthusiastic police leadership encourages appropriate communication and community interventions. The emphasis is on community strengths and learning from weaknesses. Once the police communication and trust factors are in place, the community is in an improved position to protect itself. Then, criminal activity is reduced, because positive community relations are in place, and the police are not alone. When the police communicate the right strategic message, they can earn support and citizen cooperation.

CHANNELS OF COMMUNICATION

Police messages are generally transmitted through the most efficient and effective channels of communication. Channels of communication may include: (1) speaking (as in meetings), (2) e-mail, (3) telephone conversations, (4) presentations, and, most typically, (5) informal discussions. Written letters and memorandums, especially e-mail, can lead to miscommunication.

Messages should not be sent in haste and without careful consideration. Emotional responses may lead to regrets; therefore, positive leaders delay communication until thoughts are securely in place. Text messaging and e-mails are common events that can easily lead to unfortunate emotional conflict.

Messages must be mentally decoded and understood by officers; therefore, vague comments have the potential to be misinterpreted by the receiver. In addition, many social and communication issues may interrupt or distort the intended message. Positive leaders ask the question: How will this message impact the receiver?

Sometimes, denial can prevent the message from being received. In other situations, officers may not understand the message, perhaps the result of poor listening skills or perceptions. In tactical situations, these concerns can lead to adverse consequences, even serious injury or death.

One possibility for misinterpretation: the leader engaged in faulty or unclear communication. For example, miscommunication can occur when leaders do not speak in full sentences, and officers transfer the communication to the wrong context or situation. Communication clarity remains essential to the feedback and compliance process.

One advantage of receiver clarification: the importance of the message is communicated. In addition, officers are more likely to comply with the plan or the leader's direction. Officers respond to clear, concise, and easy-to-understand communication or orders.

One way of affirming communication: ask officers if they understand the order. Give officers opportunities for clarification and feedback. Then ask them to repeat the message. This assures that the message is understood and the content can produce the desired results. Effective leaders cannot assume that messages are understood, especially in high-stress, emergency situations.

LEADERSHIP AND FEEDBACK

The essence of problem-oriented policing is input and feedback. Negative feedback from officers and leaders, to commanders, may present formidable challenges. Positive police leaders do not view negative feedback or alternatives offered as disloyalty.

Constructing solutions that address department problems requires participation and cooperation without the fear of consequences. Problem-solving requires brainstorming without the fear of adverse penalty. Effective participants lower their defensive stance and remain open to new and innovative ideas. Leadership confidence must stem from a personal sense of strength, not insecurity, blind spot, or fear of the unknown.

Creative ideas will emerge from officers in the scanning and analysis phases of the SARA planning model. Cooperation, loyalty, and support benefit the department. Credit police officers for the contributions they make. Publicly highlight an officer's personal achievements, ideas, and outstanding accomplishments.

In most instances, shared decision-making enhances the problem-solving process. Inadequate feedback is the primary reason for unsatisfactory or poor police performance. Officers, at all levels, need appropriate feedback. Police officers who do not understand new role behaviors are not going to meet standards or conform to new requirements.

REAL-TIME FEEDBACK

Communication is not necessarily a two-way process; sometimes officers may not understand or "interpret" the message. Police supervisors can eliminate many performance problems by providing personal on-the-spot feedback. If officer performance does not improve, then repeat the contact. Avoid personal remarks or demeaning behaviors; maintain positive communication.

Police leaders build their reputation and abilities to command when seizing communication initiatives. Police leaders that communicate effectively enhance officer welfare and gain respect. Leaders need followers, and followers merit effective leaders who communicate well.

Excellent communication encourages mutual understanding. Communication is not simply: (1) messenger sender and (2) message receiver. Communication thrives on feedback. Emotional components can create considerable distortion, misunderstanding, and confusion. Misinterpretation or deliberate message distortion is always a possibility. Refer to Figure 5-3 for an example of a Positive Feedback Loop.

Successful police leaders praise excellent performance. Communication can be (1) positive, (2) emotionally neutral, or (3) degrading and negative. One positive example: "Your police POP performance is outstanding." Effective leaders communicate using the positive and neutral approach and avoid emotional/negative statements.

Candid police leaders share relevant information and essential facts. Open communication avoids resentment in the long-run. Police leaders, communicating in a reliable, honest, and dependable manner, gain officer acceptance. Officers appreciate leaders who are predictable, persistent, and consistent.

Credibility helps police leaders succeed as communicators and ensures officers will listen respectfully to their messages. Confident and positive leadership delivers messages in a credible manner. These leaders are personable, supportive, and possess superior judgment skills.

Figure 5-3. Positive Feedback Loop

IMPROVING POLICE PRESENTATIONS

Leadership audience presentations require clarity and strong delivery. The message should inspire confidence and provide direction. Excellent presentations are the result of preparation and practiced speaking skills. Presentations need to be structured and rehearsed to obtain the maximum effect.

Even the most excellent presentation will not succeed if the speaker does not connect with their audience. Powerful messages are sometimes displaced by competing distractions. Most audience members have a short attention span, approximately twelve minutes. Therefore, keep the message brief and limited, to no more than three basic points.

The golden rule of communication: most audiences will remember best what they hear early in the speaker's presentation. In addition, they will likely remember repeated messages.

Communications experts refer to this as the principle of primacy, recent information, and repetition. This means that speakers attempt to make important points early, and repeat them at the end of the presentation.

Repetition on key points can be quite effective when speaking to an audience. One of best rules of public speaking states: Tell them what you are going to tell them. Tell them, and tell them again what you just told them. At this point of the presentation, the speaker emphasizes what they want the audience to remember, and act on.

Focus on the essentials of the message. Avoid making too many points and using repetitive examples. Eliminate material that clouds the message and appears as off-message digressions. The ideal presentation will last long enough to deliver the message and not one moment longer. The shorter the speech, the more likely it will achieve message objectives. Drawn-out presentations have the potential to wear the audience down, causing them to lose focus.

Remember to track audience response, and do not read verbatim from a script. Reading is the fastest way to lose audience attention. A few words, in large red fonts on cue cards, will help encourage the speaker's memory. The purpose of rehearsal: learn the material, and refer to brief notes only as necessary.

For the best results: select objectives, analyze your potential audience, and focus on your message. Effective speakers are forceful and maintain eye contact with audience members. This requires scanning the audience and making eye contact with as many listeners as possible.

Eye contact will create the image of a creative presentation and spontaneity. Moreover, it keeps the speaker on message and prevents losing the key message. Manner and attitude are more important than the factual presentation. Understanding the message material will permit strong eye contact and build a personal impression and connection.

Visual aids simply reinforce a superior performance. Power-Point can augment the police leader's presentation; however, reading the visual verbatim diverts attention from the speaker. The best visuals are inadequate substitutes for ineffective messages. Police leaders are responsible for persuasive and compelling presentations. Finally, never deliver an unprepared presentation.

COMMUNICATION: MISSION REQUIREMENTS

There are a number of detractions in high-profile and action-oriented police responses. Emergency or crisis information requires command control communication and mission essential requirements. Mission-oriented policing focuses on strategic goals and objectives, which are essential to successful outcomes. Police leaders role model compassion and concern for the officer first, then enthusiasm for mission requirements follows.

Officers comply and increase performance when they know exactly what their position requires and what is expected from the leader. Officers may fail to comply or perform at the task because the leader did not communicate effectively. Perhaps the officer(s) simply did not understand the message. Positive leaders avoid ambiguous and incomplete orders, thereby eliminating officer noncompliance.

Superior police leadership provides the path-goal plan for execution, guideline procedures, and empowering officers to problem-solve. The military operations order is an excellent example of police leadership crisis management and critical incident operations. Examine the modified military format for policing applications in the Problem-Solving Corner below.

PROBLEM-SOLVING CORNER: STAFF BRIEFING

The staff briefing provides a technique for communication, receiving feedback, and event analysis. The briefing allows for a systematic way of explaining the situation. Briefings communicate the problem in an organized manner that addresses the issues concerning a specific crime problem.

1. **Analysis of the Situation**
   a. Audience
      i. How many are there?
      ii. Nature
         (1) Who composes the audience?
         (2) Who are the ranking members?
      iii. What are their official positions?
      iv. Where are they assigned?
      v. How much professional knowledge of the subject do they have?

      vi. Are they generalists or specialists?

      vii. What are their interests?

      viii. What are their personal preferences?

      ix. What is the anticipated reaction?

  b. Purpose and Type

      i.   Information briefing: (to inform)

      ii.. Decision briefing: (to obtain decision)

      iii. Mission briefing: (to review important details)

      iv. Staff briefing: (to exchange information)

  c. Subject

      i.   What is the specific subject?

      ii. What is the desired coverage?

      iii. How much time will be allocated?

  d. Physical Facilities

      i.   Where will the briefing be presented?

      ii. What arrangements will be required?

      iii. What are the visual aid facilities?

      iv. What are the deficiencies?

      v.   What actions are needed to overcome deficiencies?

2. **Schedule of Preparatory Effort**

  a. Complete analysis of the situation

  b. Prepare preliminary outline

  c. Determine requirements for training aids, assistants, and recorders

  d. Edit or redraft

  e. Schedule rehearsals (facilities, critiques)

  f. Arrange for final review by responsible authority

3. **Constructing the Briefing**

  a. Collect Materials

      i.   Research

      ii. Become familiar with subject

      iii. Collect authoritative opinions and facts

  b. Prepare First Draft

      i.   State problem (if necessary)

      ii. Isolate key points (facts)

      iii. Identify courses of action

      iv. Analyze and compare courses of action ... State advantages and disadvantages

      v.   Determine conclusions and recommendations

   vi. Prepare draft outline
   vii. Include visual aids
   viii. Fill in appropriate material
   ix. Review with appropriate authority
 c. Revise First Draft and Edit
   i. Make sure that facts are important and necessary
   ii. Include all necessary facts
   iii. Include answers to anticipated questions
   iv. Polish material
 d. Plan Use of Visual Aids
   i. Check for simplicity—readability
   ii. Develop method for use
 e. Practice
   i. Rehearse (with assistants and visual aids)
   ii. Polish
   iii. Isolate key points
   iv. Commit outline to memory
   v. Develop transitions
   vi. Use definitive words
 f. Follow-Up
   i. Ensure understanding
   ii. Record decision
   iii. Inform proper authorities

Source: The information contained above is adapted from United States Army Field Manual 101-5, Staff Organization and Operations, 31 May 1997.

COMMUNICATION: INFORMATION SHARING

Problem-oriented organizations will target specific information, sharing formal and informal communication requirements. Organizational structure reflects the formal communication structure. Therefore, ranks within the organizational hierarchy have position and communication power.

Police officers discover information that their commanders do not know. Commanders need to build formal and informal communication systems that ensure that this information is part of the problem-solving and decision-making process. Officer ideas and imagination place them in an excellent position to provide communication feedback and solutions to street crime events.

Innovative communication strategies view police officers as reliable street leaders. Police leaders and aligned support systems

serve officers in the field and community. Positive police commanders need to develop an intelligence communication structure
throughout the department.

Leader communication with officers assists in shaping a
climate of openness. When leaders do not communicate, officers
may feel undervalued and unappreciated. However, communication balance is essential. Leaders understand the need to share
information that is appropriate for disclosure. Intelligence information must meet the basic "need to know" and proper
"security clearance" requirements.

Effective police leaders consider information-sharing consequences. Unproductive outcomes result when officers are not
properly informed. When communication is not clear, officers
may fill-in the gaps, creating rumor and further distortion. Over
communication is superior to under communication, especially in
critical or terrorist incidents.

Police officers become concerned when they feel they are
operating in an information vacuum. POP team meetings provide
opportunities to dispel myths, rumors, and misinformation. Team
meetings provide prospects for dealing with specific problems,
discussion of issues, and shared understanding.

FOCUS POINTS

Positive police leadership is the most important consideration
in communication and directly affects feedback. Leadership communication relates to a specific target audience and communicated
message essentials. The most common opportunity for miscommunication is during deployment and serious emergency and
critical incident responses. The most effective messages are:
concrete and positive. Strong police messages are offensive, not
defensive.

Police leadership necessitates clear communication messages
and active listening to be effective. The facts are not sufficient;
persuasion requires addressing emotional components. Once the
emotional cord is struck, then the audience will pay attention.
The message must be true, the whole truth, and nothing but the
truth.

Effective communication requires understanding audience
needs, anxieties, and motivation. How might the information

make a difference in their lives? Targeting specific planning and execution requirements means tailoring the message.

Police public messages are sensitive and represent an expression of sincere concern for the community. Identifying with the concerns of community citizens, patrons, and clients is essential to the effectiveness of the message.

Effective messages are not totally about the police agenda, they are about citizen or civic group audience concerns. Effective messages emphasize that the police agency cares, especially when there is a crisis or critical incident. The emphasis is on commitment to take appropriate action. The police message must ring true in the ears of listeners.

Effective police leader communication requires a clear message that can be understood by officers. Leader credibility is important. Communicating means that the leader's actions are consistent with the verbal content. Police leaders are accountable for the communication messages they send.

The police leader's credibility exists in a prism, which is reflected in officer beliefs. Officers must believe that the leader is trustworthy and the message is reliable. Officers must have confidence in the police leader's expertise and messages. Leaders, who demonstrate trust, alleviate doubt about communication messages.

CONCLUSION

Communication clarity allows for correct feedback and officer potential to meet police leader requirements. Police communication is not just about delivering information; effective communication reaches out and meets community needs. Police leaders respect audience values, and their message must reverberate with their emotional concerns.

CHAPTER 6
POSITIVE PROBLEM-SOLVING TRAINING

"The change creates three specific needs: (1) to convey a clear understanding of the overall concept of problem-oriented policing as a way of thinking about police function; (2) to equip officers to identify and analyze problems and to develop effective responses to them; and (3) to convey knowledge to officers about the most common substantive problems that they are expected to handle and to alert them to the issues involved."

— Herman Goldstein

The introduction of the dramatic change of the problem-solving approach has major implications for training programs.

Positive police executives and commanders, middle managers, sergeants, and officers encourage continuous teaching cycles and learning opportunities. The top echelon of a police organization is responsible for creating an active learning culture. This strategic shift is to learning opportunities that emphasize the human resource potential of everyone in the police agency.

The problem-solving journey unleashes the power of civilians and officers to think critically. Teachable moments are secured in the field, and problem-solving meetings take place daily. Instructional cycles are connected to the reinforcement of problem-solving goals and objectives. The police organizational maturity and development rises to new heights; everyone is open to learning.

CHAPTER FOCUS

The purpose of this chapter is to describe a diverse police approach to creative training. Every member of the police organization is expected to provide guidance and instruction throughout the organization and community. Learning occurs in both directions: leaders/instructors learn from their officers through the exchange of information and feedback.

OVERVIEW: TRAINING

Traditionally, training is the bond that brings police officers together as a team and helps facilitate superior community service. Police training is critical to survival, in a demanding and sometimes dangerous employment setting. Generally, police agencies provide four types of training: (1) entry-level police academy training, (2) Field Training Officer (FTO), (3) roll call training, and (4) specialized training.

These four basic training programs are only part of the diverse training cycles, which support POP police operations. The new approach to training includes: a willingness to learn from every member of the department. This approach offers opportunities for mutual growth, development, and self-directed learning. Training is continuous at every level of command; everyone is a trainer.

Teaching new ways of examining community problems and providing goals that provide insight into the minds of officers offer potential solutions. Teaching and inspiring officers to pursue those goals characterize the essence of leadership. The constant police leadership objective: teach officers the need to share knowledge and improve motivation to achieve those goals.

In this fast-moving knowledge and technical age, brain power is more important than muscle power. Problem-solving skills demand well-trained officers that understand what needs to be accomplished. The POP approach requires training at every level of the police organization. Instructors address training needs: knowledge is a critical asset. The dissemination of knowledge allows officers to operate independently without detailed instructions from the chain of command.

POLICE STAR LEADERSHIP PERFORMERS

Police star leadership performers understand the value of developing officer training and POP skills. Positive police leaders are obligated to develop emotional intelligence (EQ) training for officers and civilians. This goal is accomplished through effective police leadership interaction and training. Police leaders who engage this responsibility can develop winning teams for their department. This basic leadership requirement focuses police energy and encourages officers to follow through and stay the course.

The star performer leader offers a mission that is inspiring and worthy of achieving through training goals that stretch officer learning abilities. Finding teachable moments and unique transition points offers maximum opportunities to develop new learning strategies. The learning and training process is best oriented to police officer work and field experience.

PROBLEM-SOLVING FIELD TRAINING

Building a training police organization does not require a supreme effort; however, it does require a new approach to training management. There are some distractions to creating a total learning environment. Many pieces of the training puzzle need to be reformulated from the lock-step instructional model. Moreover, the correct pieces of a diverse learning approach need to be implemented to achieve training synchronization.

Training during the course of down-time prepares officers to handle community problems in real-time. The real threat to police officers: a critical incident. However, leadership and training save lives. The proactive POP-trained team focuses on goals and objectives, central to successful mission accomplishment.

Police leadership is enhanced by continuous POP field learning and training cycles. Police agencies that envelop their organizations with diverse training requirements for the POP mission enhance successful solutions. Problem-solving training is continuous and not reliant on yearly training schedules. Every officer becomes a trainer, and cross-training of the related problem-solving skills, a daily exchange. For example refer to Figure 6-1 for an illustration of Spontaneous Field Training.

New POP problem-solving requirements stipulate that police agencies become a total training environment. The difference of moving beyond lock-step training suggests that leaders determine the principles behind POP strategies. Once achieved, leaders determine appropriate actions and how to communicate them into teachable goals and objectives. This requires integrating various elements of the POP into teachable principles.

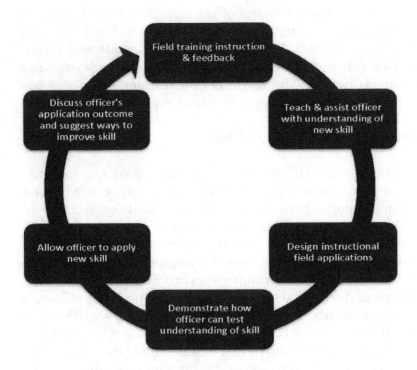

Figure 6-1. Spontaneous Field Training

BUILDING THE TRAINING CLIMATE

Excellent police POP training requires officers to participate in the critical-thinking and problem-solving process, skills required in the field and that are the essence of every police training program. Police officers should be confronted with real-world POP situations they may encounter in their communities. The emphasis should be on active learning based on field scenarios, role playing, and learning simulations.

What does excellent POP training accomplish? Excellent training produces officers who successfully perform POP mission requirements and enables police officers to understand where they are going. The training process provides the skills for accomplishing essential field tasks. Police officers must learn to meet challenges similar to those in their community.

POP training must be performance oriented, not classroom oriented. The lecture method should be a small part of the training unit. When the lecture method is used, the trainer should follow-up with a field demonstration. The demonstration should include officer participation and interaction. For police training to be meaningful, it must facilitate active learning, not passive learning.

Active learning is more than instructor/lecture oriented; it requires interaction between instructors and officers as well as interaction with other learners in the classroom. Encouraging peer interaction allows officers to learn from each other. Active learning encourages an exchange of ideas and feedback, the latter essential to learning. Critical thinking and problem-solving encourage officer involvement in the feedback and learning process. Role playing and learning simulations maximize instructor and student feedback.

Positive police leadership and POP training opportunities originate primarily from community policing responses. Formal training programs will likely represent a smaller portion of the learning curve in the future. The basic POP training strategy should be lecture/theory first. POP instructional content offers opportunities for role-playing scenarios, followed by a critique and discussion. The performance-oriented training should approximate field conditions.

Problem-oriented training is about diverse informal scheduling, timely information, and field training. Building an active training/learning police organization requires a multifaceted approach to teaching core competencies of a policing and problem-solving approach. Police leaders become role model trainers who coach and mentor their officers well.

Police training becomes an interactive model not predetermined to a specific time and place. The police agency emphasizes a total organizational approach to training, which involves continuous cycles of training and informational communication exchanges. Police training is ongoing and concerns the adaptable exchange of knowledge. This training exchange at every level allows officers to stay ahead of the learning curve.

Everyone becomes a learner with a sense of humility. Leaders not only perform as instructors, they learn from their officers. There is no clear line of demarcation in the new, fast-changing environment and the POP problem-solving requirements. Critical incidents are fast-paced responses, which require decision-making at the lowest level of tactical operations.

The leadership model of the future will emphasize a police leader's ability to accept criticism and achieve growth and development through adversity. The learning process and self-criticism can generate the necessary openness, energy, and excitement to stimulate POP teams to win, while confronting dangerous conditions.

BENEFITS OF POP TRAINING

POP training builds human resources and the motivation to perform the mission. It also assists in defeating obstacles that prevent team building. For example, problems such as personnel turnover, potential racial tension, and drug/alcohol abuse make it difficult to build teams.

Training skills often provide the "glue" that holds the organization together. The establishment of POP training programs can help improve respect for race, gender, and individual differences. This kind of training can help to encourage and maintain discipline and social cohesion.

Men and women training together and working toward common POP goals are far less susceptible to tension from within and outside the police organization. Well-trained officers are more likely to cooperate under stress and perform the POP mission successfully. They develop a winning attitude and are more confident when performing POP tasks and objectives.

MILITARY TEAM TRAINING APPLICATIONS

Effective POP deployment strategies and tactics are usually target specific. The important outcome: being in the right places, at the approximate time of offenses, and targeting offenders. POP training supports community problem-solving and CompStat tactical operations.

Special Weapons and Tactics (SWAT) operations require instantaneous decisions. Police operations may approximate military operations, which demand excellent training and coaching. Ultimately, in real-time tactical situations, officers are independent decision-makers.

The war in Afghanistan riveted on the United States Special Operations Forces (SOF) and their battlefield operations. Military personnel in the field were authorized to seek targets of opportunity and make field combat judgments. The command

and control headquarters gave the broadest mission parameters; however, the military personnel made independent, real-time decisions.

Field soldiers made decisions; they were responsible for teaching central command and others in the field. Thereby informing and educating those with a need to know about battlefield conditions. The learning occurred at every level. This was made possible through realistic training cycles and candid decision-making at every level of command. Lessons learned are passed on to commanders for future doctrine and training changes.

This instructional/learning model is related to the Navy SEALs and Army Special Forces and offers a total training environment. Everyone contributes after an operation to determine the facts. The purpose: a brainstorming after-action report. The goal: active listening, respecting everyone's opinion, regardless of rank, and learning from the experience. Special OPS examine the mission and answer basic questions about what was done right and what the teams can improve on. These special Navy SEALs and SOF units represent classic examples of coaching/teaching organizations.

The military represents the ultimate command and control organization. When examining Navy SEALs, Army Special Forces, Army Rangers, and other special operations units, this stereotype does not prevail. Militarily, special operation commands are superior coaching and teaching organizations. Leaders must problem-solve and make instantaneous decisions without contacting commanders. They respond to worldwide hot spots.

Police team leadership and training require smaller groups (approximately ten officers). The officers must have the ability to establish relationships, which encourage frequent communication and interaction. Effective police teams unfold because of their need for cooperation and interdependence, which stems from the appreciation of each member's abilities and training skill level. Informal POP leadership occurs in a team-training context regardless of rank or position.

DIVERSE LEARNING CYCLES

Large civilian police departments represent similar paramilitary learning cycles and obstacles. The long chain of command interferes with real-time operations. An adaptation of the military team format may offer some solutions. Assigning a training specialist to each POP training team would assist in recycling teaching and improving the learning curve. Refer to Figure 6-2 for comparison, analysis, and adaptation from a military team, to a possible police POP Training Team.

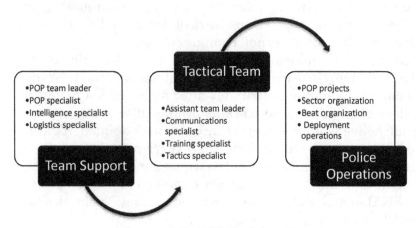

Figure 6-2. POP Training Teams

Instructional and learning cycles cascade down the chain of command through each organizational unit. These instructional/ teaching cycles allow special operating teams to implement new elements and modify the operation. The instruction/learning is also recycled back up the chain of command from operating teams. Police teams are continuously customized for the POP mission; training behaviors and tactics evolve from field experiences.

POP teams can serve community problem-solving functions or be deployed as tactical teams. Cross-training and POP learning teams encourage questioning and interchange of problem-solving strategies, at every level of the organization. Disciplined POP teams create a high level of trust. Learning and training curves improve when everyone's opinion is respected, regardless of rank.

CRISIS AND CRITICAL INCIDENT TRAINING

Police agencies respond in three phases to crisis and critical incident management: (1) preparation, (2) response, and (3) recovery. Effective training and preparation for crisis management planning require continuous evaluation. Planning necessitates validating the plan through training and realistic performance exercises.

Training and continuous plan updating necessitates modifying responses based on new information, and quickly changing conditions. The remedial response phase involves training, activating, and implementing tactical planning in real-time. The recovery phase requires returning to normal operations after the emergency or critical incident acute phase.

Reviewing the after-action briefing provides proper feedback and the means for modifying the training planning process. The examination of facts, after the critical or emergency incident, reviews performance and suggests future improvements. Lessons learned in the crisis stage assist police agencies in future emergency scenarios. More importantly, lessons may help anticipate future emergencies and encourage additional innovative responses.

Training, planning, and all related emergency circumstances demand authenticating what created the crisis scenario. The crisis plan is a systematic approach, which provides a focusing point where leaders can assess potential crisis scenarios. Planning permits leaders to gain insight into the appropriate internal and external community response(s).

PROBLEM-SOLVING CORNER: POP TRAINING

A formal training curriculum should proceed in the formalization stage prior to initiating POP programs. The training philosophy guides POP curriculum mandates. A philosophical statement describes the basic tenants of POP programming. Philosophy emphasis is on critical thinking, problem-solving, and meeting community needs. Statement tenants describe the need to cooperate with stakeholders, patrons, and clients.

Training goals describe general themes that drive POP training objectives. Objectives contain a task, standard, and criterion. Objectives implement the broad goals. The task describes training, and behavioral outcomes. The standard measures successful task accomplishment.

POP Training Philosophy

The COPPS philosophy is the dominant theme. There is a direct strategic connection between COP and POP that equals COPPS. The problem-solving process demands community participation and cooperation. POP is the strategic component for addressing effective solutions to community problems. Problem-solving applies the SARA method of planning, which seeks to prevent and eliminate crime. COP establishes community connections and the necessary support for POP.

POP Training Goals

POP learning goals include the following basic primary components:

1. Grouping incidents as problems is the first requirement. Move beyond handling criminal incidents. Identify incidents and related problem symptoms.

2. Focusing on substantive problems provides direction. Identify recurring problems that are substantive problems.

3. Effectiveness is the first consideration, but not the only one. Effectiveness requires defining what problem is worthy of identification and establishing priorities.

4. Staff/line officers identify the collection system to analyze data for potential remedial actions. Identify how incidents are connected and related. Establish a collection system that includes crime and service statistics. Other information-gathering systems include telephone questionnaires and surveys. Conduct offender and victim interviews.

5. Redefine problems through accurate crime analysis. Precise problem definitions are essential to successful POP programming, and resolutions. The labeling process will ultimately determine the level of priority.

6. Who has or should be interested in the problem? The first step is to determine who the victims are, those being harmed indirectly, and the social costs. This is essential to developing a successful POP action plan.

7. Customize remedial actions. Crime problems are specific to the police agency, community, and neighborhood. The methods for resolving crime problems must be specific. While outside applications may have value, they should be tailor-made and adjusted to address the specific crime problem.

8. Taking the offensive means avoiding the defensive and reactive posture. The first step involves the initial identification of the problem and systematic analysis. The second step involves an active program for educating the public. The third step requires identifying community problems and referring them to the proper source or agency.

9. Improve decision visibility. Problem-solving requires explaining the rationale for the decision. High visibility and open communication assists in public cooperation.

10. Evaluation and feedback requires multilevel procedures that are part of every step along the pathway to successful solutions. Evaluation supports all SARA components. This means making incremental adjustments and improvements along the pathway. Reliable assessment and evaluation describe if the police agency's original grouping of problems was correct. Without this component, POP will not arrive at valid solutions, which point to future directions.

POP Training Objectives

POP fundamentals include the following practices and related learning objectives:

→ Appraise substantive community problems.
→ Identify the systematic nature of recurring offenses.
→ Inquire systematically into the nature and causes of crime.

→ Appraise community interests in resolving related crimes.
→ Identify special interest groups related to crimes.
→ Assess current police responses to related crimes.
→ Identify the systematic search for tailor-made solutions.
→ Apply evaluation and assessment procedures to measure the effectiveness of solutions.

Program Needs Assessment

Training needs assessments address basic POP training requirements. Goals and objectives are formulated and evaluated as part of the training needs assessment process. Training goals and objectives meet established standards: (1) specific, (2) measurable set of criteria, and (3) time table for achievement and application. POP training program development requires revisions based on needs assessments.

Program Evaluation

POP training evaluation represents a continuous process that determines effectiveness. The officers' understanding of POP training goals and objectives is best evaluated in the field. Measuring performance initially occurs when comparing the officer's effectiveness with pre-training and post-training assessments in field follow-up procedures.

PROBLEM-SOLVING CORNER: COMMUNITY TRAINING

Police agencies frequently provide training to enhance crime intervention, prevention, and community relations. Police agencies typically engage in community training programs. Generally, these programs include bicycle safety, driver education, Neighborhood Watch, and senior citizen police academy programs. The community training and educational programs cited offer research outcomes by Michael S. Scott and Herman Goldstein:

> *Police have long been involved in systematically conveying information to the public on how to prevent crime. They do this through presentation, brochures, and a variety of other programs. Some of these efforts are aimed broadly at the public; others are targeted at specific*

constituencies. Educational messages and programs are directed either at potential victims, instructing them on how to avoid being victimized, or at potential offenders, instructing them on how to avoid offending.

Scott and Goldstein describe a police community training program concerning sexual assault and teenagers: San Diego, California police analysis found that a high percentage of sexual assault cases were acquaintance rapes involving teenagers. By examining and analyzing the relevant case files, the sexual assault unit identified the patterns of conduct that led to such assaults and then constructed a school-based curriculum designed to inform students on reducing the risk of victimization.

The initiative produced brochures—different ones for males and females—that sought to inform students, using language and scenarios familiar to them, about what constitutes acquaintance rape, how women can avoid being victimized by it, and how men can avoid being accused of it.

Scott and Goldstein cite an excellent example of a landlord tenant police community training program. Based on the analysis of their experience in dealing with crime and disorder in apartment complexes, some police agencies have developed remedial manuals for both property owners and tenants, and sponsor seminars where these materials are presented. The goal is to encourage both property owners and tenants to assume more responsibility for conditions in their housing units by employing specific prevention measures, such as the enforcement of occupancy restrictions and prohibitions against illegal activity, control over entry and public areas, the installation and operation of security systems, and so forth.

In many instances, persuading property owners and managers to lease only to responsible tenants, to enforce the rules that govern proper behavior on the premises, and to design and maintain properties in ways that discourage problems can be more effective than criminal law enforcement.

Scott and Goldstein describe a police community training program concerning the selling alcohol to teenagers: Concerned about the problem of underage drinking, police in Plano, Texas developed an informational presentation for the owners and managers of stores licensed to sell alcoholic beverages outlining the measures that could be taken to help store clerks comply with law prohibiting the sale of alcohol to minors.

Although stern warnings and enforcement were essential components of the initiative, police found that some clerks were confused about the law and about how to detect fraudulent attempts to purchase alcohol. Consequently, the informational programs were more than a way of issuing a polite warning; they in fact helped people who were inclined to obey the law to do so.

Scott and Goldstein call attention to the community training themes and communication: Central to all of these efforts, however, is the fact that those to whom the message is directed are in a position to take actions that will protect themselves from either victimization or arrest. Such educational materials and presentations are generally low-key; one can take the advice or ignore it. Educational messages to potential offenders adopt a helpful rather than a warning tone; they are aimed at people who are inclined to obey the law, but who might offend out of ignorance or carelessness.

Source: Michael S. Scott, and Herman Goldstein, Shifting and Sharing Responsibility for Public Safety Problems, U. S. Department of Justice: Community Oriented Policing Services (COPS) (Washington DC: GPO, 2005).

In summary, community training programs are an essential part of police programming and POP problem-solving. The POP and problem-solving approach allow police agencies to assess and evaluate neighborhoods and their respective resources. Thus, when police agencies shift some of these local crime prevention efforts to community organizations and residents, it improves effectiveness. Communities and local neighborhoods must accept responsibility for specific social problems under their control. The police cannot prevent, suppress, or control crime alone.

Successful police organizations are responsive, flexible, and adjust to the changing state of community affairs. Finding teachable moments and the learning point of view open the opportunity door. Leaders seize the opening to become trainers for rapidly changing community problems and receive community feedback. Positive leaders take the opportunity to learn from their failures, pick up the pieces, and move on to successful conclusions.

PROFESSIONAL TRAINING/ASSISTANCE

The International Association of Chiefs of Police (IACP) has proven to be a valuable asset in training and preparing law enforcement officials for serving citizens and police agencies in these challenging, sometimes unpredictable, and rapid moving times. Their planning and policy initiatives contribute to a wide variety of topics and concerns. IACP provides current advances in police leadership, management, and training.

IACP can assist in the reorganization of police agencies coping with modern paradigm changes. IACP's innovative operational practices and organizational research benefit state and local police agencies. IACP maintains an active professional role in the exchange of ideas and information on successful police leadership and training management strategies.

The IACP continues to offer technical training seminars and publications that explore recent scientific and crime fighting developments. *Police Chief Magazine* offers considerable insight into every facet of crime fighting initiatives. This excellent professional journal is a must-read for law enforcement professionals. This IACP publication strives for scholarly articles that emphasize applied research on numerous policing topics. The articles range from national to international topics, which illustrate the most recent leadership strategies and police problem-solving strategies.

FOCUS POINTS

Positive police leaders find teachable moments to convey their knowledge and learn from their officers. Experimental POP learning models ensure that officers understand mental and behavioral skills. These leaders are open to new ideas.

Positive leaders use learning opportunities to communicate those ideas and values to officers. This form of instruction improves leader self-awareness and serves as the starting point for revisions and improvements in problem-solving solutions.

Officers learn quickly and retain more information by means of POP problem-solving applications. The concept of diverse and universal field learning and training encourages development of POP problem-solving skills.

New skills can be learned by experimenting with innovative POP initiatives. Officers learn from direct application of POP objectives in the community. Every member of the police agency is a trainer and learner in the feedback cycle.

POP and SARA models promote opportunities to engage in personal observations. This training model encompasses planning, POP instruction, and result assessment.

Officers are given opportunities to practice skills and training feedback on how well they are performing. The next learning opportunity presents itself in field opportunities to apply training skills and receive community feedback.

After considerable refection on training experiences, field lessons learned require fine-tuning, and the training cycle continues. Police officers, who desire successful POP outcomes, seek training and field application opportunities.

CONCLUSION

Police organizations that have a diverse instructional/ teaching feedback structure enhance POP operations. Excellent training in police agencies offers the best option to meet future challenges. Police agencies that provide diverse training strategies and operational training provide multifaceted learning opportunities. New and diverse instructional strategies and learning modalities serve as a foundation for meeting the new POP requirements.

PART III
POSITIVE POLICE PLANNING AND COACHING

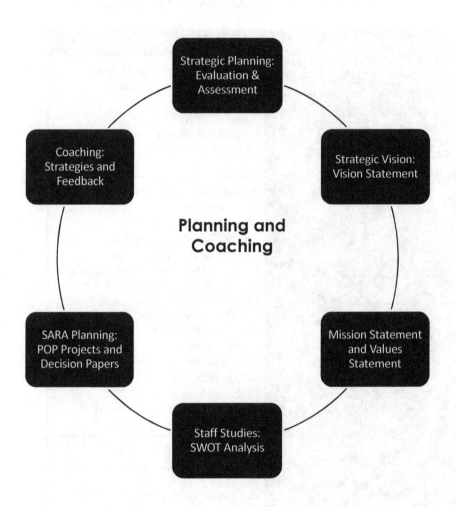

Strategic Planning: Evaluation & Assessment

Strategic Vision: Vision Statement

Coaching: Strategies and Feedback

Planning and Coaching

Mission Statement and Values Statement

SARA Planning: POP Projects and Decision Papers

Staff Studies: SWOT Analysis

POSITIVE POLICE PLANNING AND COACHING

Leadership Foundations	Guidepost Behaviors
Describe the POP vision: Positive Police Strategic planning Vision statement Mission statement Value statement **EQ and SWOT analysis**	**Define strategic pathway:** Define strategic objectives Define strategic goals Commit procedures Conduct staff studies Perform evaluation and assessment
SARA planning: Positive police leadership Telling the story POP field analysis Problem-solving procedures	**Scanning, analysis, response & assessment** Write POP objectives Apply SMART principles Develop POP action plan Conduct POP project appraisals
POP projects: Positive police leadership POP components POP themes POP project stages POP project management	**Coordination:** Partners, clients, supporters Basic components Specific scope Specific schedule Required resources POP statement Define stages, management & evaluation procedures
Coaching POP projects: Positive police leadership building trust Coaching and EQ Active listening Clarification Feedback	**Establish relationship:** Identify POP performance behaviors Explain need for POP improvement Discuss timeline for completion Expectation and performance requirements Praise correct behaviors

CHAPTER 7
POSITIVE STRATEGIC PLANNING, EVALUATION, AND ASSESSMENT

"Analysis requires the acquisition of detailed inform-ation about offenders, victims, and others who may be involved in a problem, the time of occurrence, loca-tions, details about the physical environment, the motivations, gains and losses of all involved parties, and the results of current responses."
— Herman Goldstein

Positive leadership is the result of excellent decision-making. Police leaders and officers are constantly involved in the decision-making process; they make more decisions than corporate execu-tives. Some of the decision-making is short-term and immediate. For example, tactical critical incidents and emergency responders initiate prior training skills and established protocols. However, many important strategic decisions are systemic and long-term. These problem-solving decisions are best engaged during the strategic planning and evaluation phases.

Police senior leadership formulates the strategic plan, mission, related long-term goals, and objectives. Senior leadership develops the concepts for successful execution and evaluation of those responsibilities. They encourage support for creative ideas and values. Senior leaders maintain their vigilant search for enthusiasm and a competitive edge that initiates successful crime solutions.

CHAPTER FOCUS

The purpose of this chapter is to focus on Strategic Planning, Evaluation, and Assessment. The rationale is to identify the vision for future POP direction, goals, and objectives. Moreover, the con-tent outlines the function of the staff study, assessment, and evaluation procedures as a means for achieving future transitions.

OVERVIEW: STRATEGIC PLANNING

The strategic planning process requires setting long-term goals and supporting related objectives. Effective police leadership requires understanding the human dimension as well as the strategic and tactical picture. Strategic planning provides a formal and written roadmap to the future. The strategic plan is the means to chart a forward POP affirmative position for the police agency. Specifically, it defines destination and how the police department will arrive in a predetermined time frame. The plan is a strategic leadership strategy for assisting the vision of future mission destinations.

POLICE STAR LEADERSHIP PERFORMERS

Emotional intelligence (EQ) provides the primary steps for problem-solving POP strategies and decision-making. For example, controlling impulses is the perquisite for serving as a strategic policing change agent. Positive star performers understand that setting strategic goals, and identifying alternative solutions, can meet considerable resistance.

Identifying social change consequences requires understanding the emotional climate. Daniel Goleman notes that understanding the perspective of others, and what is acceptable behavior, is best understood in the behavioral norms. This requires reading nonverbal communication through eye contact, facial expressions, tone of voice, gestures, etc. Reading social clues is important to selling the strategic vision.

STRATEGIC ACCELERATION

The strategic approach incorporates seeing the "big picture," which includes police positive leadership and understanding the principles of human behavior.

Tony Jeary, in his book, *Strategic Acceleration: Success at the Speed of Life*, stresses the lightning pace of modern life. He defines three important qualities that increase strategic potential: (1) *Clarity:* the capability to get clear about what the organization wants to achieve; (2) *Focus:* the capacity to avoid distractions, and concentrate on the most important strategic outcomes; and (3) *Execution:* the competence to apply strategic communication to achieve and exceed expectations, and achieve faster results.

First Step: Complete the Staff Study; strategic information enhances clarity and focus.

Second Step: Select goals and objectives. This step requires articulation and coordination.

Third Step in the vision picture alignment process: Coordinate with action plans.

Fourth Step on the road to successful execution and advancement: Develop complementary team members.

Fifth Step: Sequence the tasking process.

Sixth Step: Assessment and evaluation.

The strategic plan includes: (1) mission and values statement, (2) description of the police agency's long-term strategic goals and objectives, (3) strategies and plans to achieve strategic goals and objectives, and, most importantly, (4) action plans to implement and secure strategic goals and objectives. The strategic plan identifies relevant factors and details that can affect purpose achievement.

Strategic planning provides police agency direction to successful implementation of ideas, concepts, and action. Components of the plan require defining answers to the following questions: (1) Where is the police agency now? (2) Where is the police agency going? (3) How will the police agency get there? and (4) How will the police agency know when it has arrived?

Strategic planning assesses motivational factors, organizational structure, and internal and external strategies. The final outcome of the strategic plan: Where does the police agency go next? Strategic planning requires excellent intelligence analysis and criminal information.

INTELLIGENCE CYCLE

Intelligence-Led Policing (ILP) is the master organizational strategy that guides the collection of raw data and criminal information in law enforcement organizations. The administration and centralization of raw intelligence data require liaison activities that accomplish synchronization and proper dissemination. The information-sharing process is expansive and coordination mandated.

Intelligence analysis is the means to collect, collate, and disseminate strategic intelligence. This kind of analysis generally focuses on relationships among persons and organizations involved in illegal and conspiratorial activities (i.e., narcotics trafficking, organized prostitution, organized or enterprise crime, gangs, terrorism, etc.).

Intelligence analysis may provide information on organized criminal activities and organizations. Intelligence analysis focuses on the trends, distribution of drugs, and activities of criminal organization members. Collation and targeting processes demand excellent analysis and improve strategic and tactical planning. Police leaders need actionable criminal intelligence that improves strategic and tactical decision-making.

Intelligence cycle fundamentals include: collection of raw data, analysis, and timely dissemination. The essential quality: accurate information analysis. Otherwise, it is merely a collation of facts and raw data. Intelligence analysis is not simply a step-by-step linear process. The analysis process is cyclic, moving in many directions, and returning to former original stages as new data becomes available.

ILP provides the coordination of criminal information that supports appropriate problem-solving solutions. Intelligence and crime analysis, together, maximize effective leadership and intelligence management solutions. A pending need exists to consolidate intelligence and crime analysis into a singular ILP intelligence/crime analysis unit.

POLICE STRATEGIC VISION

Strategic leadership addresses future opportunities that assure the department's timely arrival. Positive police leaders constantly search for methods that highlight and motivate their vision into the future. Examine the following six steps for getting there:

Step 1: Examine the existing mission and values statement's essential components. The purpose is to scrutinize transitioning fundamentals that require revision and attention. Study the current status and police strategic positioning. Examine police internal organizational requirements and external community environmental influences. Then determine what/where adjustments are required to ensure successful strategic and long-range strategies.

Step 2: Analyze the mission statement for its purpose. Define why the police agency necessitates correcting the course and changing direction. The mission statement includes community and strategic course factors. Does the mission statement reflect the police department's destination? If not, the mission statement requires rewriting to include: a newly defined destination and emphasis.

Step 3: Develop vision goals and objectives that require action and the articulation of values for officers to follow. Values clarify what the police agency stands for and serve as guideposts for officers to measure destination. Police values define beliefs that are important to core operations and arriving at the destination on time. The values statement keeps officers and civilians on a leadership pathway.

Step 4: Determine where the police department is going next. This guiding principle inspires a second question: What will the police department look like in the future? Predicting the future is difficult; however, current trends permit basic approximate assessments. This strategic assessment defines what the police agency will look like five to ten years into the future.

Step 5: Establish long-term goals that address strategic commitments and support the police agency's mission and values statements. Vision requirements include four essential areas: (1) financial, (2) police and civilian personnel, (3) customers, patrons, and clients, and (4) community. Strategies establish how the police department will deploy the agency's strengths to match community needs, avoid weaknesses, and maximize opportunities.

Step 6: Evaluation/assessment is an indispensable tool when reorienting strategic planning cycles and implementing the planning process. The evaluation process is essential when adjusting: vision, mission, goals, and objectives. Evaluation helps propose new goals and objectives that initiate new action plans. Applied evaluation research provides valid information for future applications. Refer to Figure 7-1 Strategic Planning for an illustration of the future-oriented planning approach.

THE MISSION STATEMENT

Where does vision come from? A vision originates from staff studies, POP policing, and community partnerships. The past can serve as a point of view, but analysis of the future remains essential. Vision evolves from the strategic planning process and community perspective. The chief and senior leaders initiate a strategic framework; however, planning is modified through feedback from police leaders, supervisors, and officers.

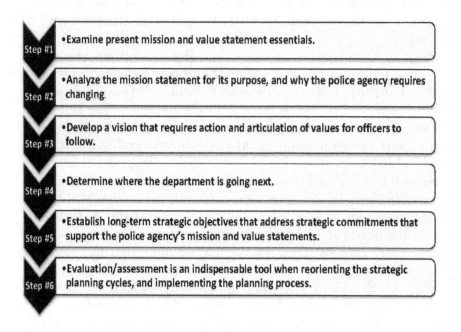

Figure 7-1. Strategic Planning

How do we implement vision? The Chief and senior leaders are responsible for coordinating police paradigms. Positive police leadership teaches police paradigms and demonstrates the correct implementation. The paradigms and mission statement are repeated until incorporated into department traditions. This clarity guides strategic planning and decision-making. Police paradigms set the foundation for change and are incorporated into the strategic planning process.

The chief and subordinates develop the mission statement to provide direction. The mission statement also demonstrates the law enforcement agency's purpose and rational. The mission statement defines: (1) acceptable attitudes, (2) conduct, and (3) performance.

Mission statement clarity is an important consideration. The mission statement documents: (1) department direction and (2) goals. Mission orientation defines: (1) purpose and (2) organization guidelines for officers to follow. A mission statement is the standard against which police leaders evaluate all paradigms, decisions, and actions.

The following mission statement is a model: *The police department will promote problem-solving policing and community solutions to crime and disorder. Police community partnerships, clients, and citizens will ultimately enhance quality policing services and public safety in the community.*

Assessing the police department's mission statement requires articulating a clear and concise foundation. The mission statement explains reasons for the police agency's existence. It provides guidance for daily police department operations. This formal statement focuses on meeting community needs and preventing crime.

The police mission statement should inspire officers to the highest level of dedication. Moreover, the statement is memorable, clear, succinct, and practical. The statement addresses police competencies related to successful mission requirements. The words are specific and core to the purpose of police goals.

The mission statement should reflect the future to maintain its relevance. Police leaders need to conduct a preliminary review of the mission statement. In addition, solicit everyone's opinion. Then successfully work in partnership to rewrite the mission statement. The police mission statement is a work in progress; the content is fluid, not fixed.

VALUES STATEMENT

The values and mission statements assist in creating an ethical climate. While the mission statement describes where the organization is going, the values statement articulates how it will get there. The values statement is a detailed guide of behaviors, which management accepts and supports within the organization. The values statement provides guidance for officer performance and defines acceptable behaviors.

Value statements are enduring, core beliefs, which characterize guiding principles. This statement describes what police officers stand for and declares strongly held convictions. These underlying assumptions influence attitudes and professional behaviors. Values represent strong convictions about policing and community service.

Values serve as strategic behaviors the police department either accepts or rejects. Core values are important to the police organization's success, and are essential to strategic goals and objectives. Policing values need to be specific to the mission statement. Essential values are generally restricted to approximately ten memorable statements.

THE VISION STATEMENT

The vision statement is a concise statement of the police department's future forecasting state, and destination. The purpose of the statement: inspire determination, motivate, and encourage police officers to reach future destinations. Mission statements motivate police agencies beyond their present status.

The description provides a strategic picture, creates excitement, enthusiasm, and encourages challenging future requirements. The description is powerful, energetic, and appealing. After reading or listening to the vision statement, officers feel a sense of purpose, and clarification regarding the right direction.

DEFINING STRATEGIC GOALS

There are significant differences between long-range strategic planning, and long-range planning. Long-range POP planning refers to the development of an action plan to accomplish a goal or goals over a period of five to ten years. The purpose of long-range POP planning: emphasize current knowledge about future conditions. The conditions appear static, understandable, and predicable for planners to accomplish their long-range goals.

The major assumption in strategic planning: the police organization must operate in a dynamic, changing set of circumstances. This approach requires that strategic planning and its related goals; operate in a constant environment of instability and social change. Strategic POP long-term goals are broadly stated vision requirements, responsive to changing conditions. Therefore, the direction of these changes are estimated and accounted for, especially in fluctuating circumstances.

Strategic POP goals are directly connected to mission and vision statements. The goals are related to strategic vision requirements and successful outcomes. In addition, supporting objectives are connected to strategic goals and lead to their successful acquisition and attainment. They are written in the action verb format.

SWOT ANALYSIS

Linking the social components for assessing the police agency's strategic POP plan and destination include: (1) defining and (2) examining strengths and weaknesses. The acronym SWOT represents: (1) Strengths, (2) Weaknesses, (3) Opportunities, and (4) Threats. Addressing these four areas is essential when assessing the police department's strategic position and defining the next destination. The foundation is based on maximizing strengths and improving weaknesses. The police department's two main goals: (1) eliminating potential threats and (2) taking advantage of existing opportunities.

SWOT meetings are future-oriented. Strategic planning groups/staff analysis should encompass three time components: (1) present, (2) short-term, and (3) long-term. The present situation will be easier to define. However, short-term analysis may emerge as being precise and long-term analysis, possibly vague. The assessment and evaluation process measures long-range goal effectiveness, synchronization, and coordination. Refer to Figure 7-2-A for an illustration of a Balance Sheet: Graphic Analysis of a Preliminary Work-Sheet Illustration.

SWOT meetings are brainstorming sessions that involve staff, commander, officers, and civilians. The goal: examine important factors that address threats and weakness. Moreover, the meeting is conducted in a manner where everyone feels comfortable sharing their opinions. SWOT factors and issues are constantly assessed and evaluated.

Conducting SWOT analysis is an integral segment of a continuing strategic planning process. An assessment of department resources and capabilities to succeed complement the strategic plan. The SWOT analysis/balance sheet is a measure of the police department's present capabilities. SWOT analyzes: (1) internal and community strengths and (2) police agency weaknesses. It also examines criminal or other threats to basic analysis requirements. SWOT analysis is connected to the threat/risk assessment process. Refer Figure 7-2-B for an illustration of POP SWOT Assessment.

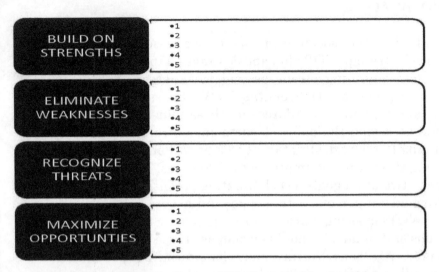

Figure 7-2-A. Balance Sheet: Graphic Analysis

STRENGTHS	WEAKNESSES
Capabilities:	*Gaps in capabilities:*
• Intelligence-Led Policing	• POP training programs
• Crime analysis	• POP team development
• Intelligence analysis	• Leadership training
• Operations analysis	• Predictability
• POP planning	• Budget constraints
• COMPSTAT operations	• Reduction in force
• GIS crime mapping	• Doing more with less
OPPORTUNITIES	**THREATS**
Tactics:	*Increasing levels of neighbor-hood crime:*
• Neighborhood Watch programs	• Drug trafficking
• Local neighborhood police sub-stations	• Robberies
• Officer interest in reducing crime	• Burglaries
• Concerned business owners	• Street prostitution
• Concerned citizens	• Businesses leaving
	• Increased drug addiction

Figure 7-2-B. POP SWOT Assessment

THREAT/RISK ASSESSMENT

Risk and threat assessments analyze terrorist and enterprise crime groups, and operations that threaten American communities. Criminal operations that directly and indirectly threaten the nation's peace and stability influence the need for intelligence analysis, and threat and risk assessments. This type of proactive intelligence analysis attempts to predict the vulnerability of the nation, communities, and infrastructure.

The concepts of threat and risk assessment overlap, and some confusion exists regarding the application of terms. Government and private sectors expose differing perspectives. Some dissimilarity arises over individual preferences, or differences and organizational needs. There are no universally accepted definitions of risk or threat assessments. Historically, the military and government applied threat analysis to terrorism and organized crime. However, more recently, government and private sectors perpetuate blending definitions of threat and risk assessment. Currently, multiple definitions or conceptual applications apply subtle differences.

The United States General Accounting Office (GAO), National Security, and International Affairs Division incorporate the following definitions of threat assessment and risk management. The former represents an intelligence approach, while the other is management oriented:

> *"Threat and risk assessments are widely recognized as valid decision support tools to establish and prioritize security program requirements. In threat analysis, the first step in determining risk, identifies and evaluates each threat on the basis of various factors, such as its capability and intent to attack an asset, the likelihood of a successful attack, and its lethality."*

The GAO cited different levels of analysis and management: "Risk management is the deliberate process of understanding 'risk'—the likelihood that a threat will harm an asset with some severity of consequences—and deciding on and implementing actions to reduce it. Risk management principles acknowledge that: (1) while risk generally cannot be eliminated, it can be reduced by enhancing protection from validated and credible threats; (2) although many threats are possible, some are more likely to occur than others; and (3) all assets are not equally critical."

Basic Field Assessment Strategies

Crime prevention surveys can provide field information concerning terrorist and criminal behavior. Crime prevention surveys can analyze the human part of the equation, and underlying foundations for criminal behavior. In addition, intelligence/criminal information can be obtained from surveillance, wiretapping, informant sources, and offender behaviors.

Physical security surveys can address the security posture with regard to lighting, building perimeter security, and access control. The goal: eliminate opportunities for terrorists and criminals to penetrate targets and critical assets. The information gleaned from physical surveys serves as the foundation for an improved security posture and eliminates risks for future offenses.

Intelligence Cycle

Field information is advanced to analysts, where it is collected, collated, and analyzed in the intelligence cycle. The information can serve as contributing factors to the strategic picture. Intelligence feedback from field officers is essential to successful threat and risk assessments. The Intelligence Cycle serves as the means to manage data or criminal information for strategic analysis and threat/risk assessment strategies.

Intelligence analysis assesses the internal characteristics of terrorists, or enterprise crime organizations, for vulnerability and interdiction points. Intelligence analyst teams identify and evaluate threats, vulnerabilities, and countermeasures to manage or reduce risks. Quantitative mathematical, qualitative analysis, and computer models generate specific threat scenarios from valid intelligence and threat data. This intelligence can then be paired with critical vulnerabilities that quantify risk probability levels. Threat and risk assessments require periodic reassessment to modify countermeasures that are appropriate and updated.

Strategic Intelligence

Strategic analysis, threat, and risk assessment reports are predictive and future oriented. The threat assessment may take the form of a warning. Eventually, the threat or risk assessment merges into a vulnerability assessment. Aggressive analysis quantifies the aggressiveness, adventurousness, and expansionist tendencies of terrorist or enterprise crime groups and their operations. The use of force and intimidation is an index of power and control themes. Analysis includes examining the use of lethal violence by a group.

Strategic intelligence estimates include information analysis of terrorist or enterprise criminal activities and future trends. Intelligence estimates are useful against transnational criminals from a disruption, interdiction, prevention, and tactical operations point of view. Historical antecedents may also precede the threat assessment report.

Intelligence estimates are a compilation of data, which measure the historical occurrence of terrorist or criminal activity and include trends and forecasts based on historical data. Finally, strategic intelligence may have different types of analysis: (1) threat assessments, (2) risk assessments, (3) vulnerability assessments, (4) aggressive analysis, and (5) warnings.

Intelligence Summary

Operational intelligence identifies the intentions of criminal adversaries. The most common definition of risk: it is the product of hazard and vulnerability. Terrorism and enterprise crime require similar approaches; however, the human dimension is fraught with difficult variables to manage.

The focus: organizational systems, network analysis, and terrorist and enterprise/organized crime criminals' abilities to act on various political or criminal scenarios. Most importantly, the Intelligence Cycle, and risk and threat assessments help measure the level of aggressiveness and lethality that threaten the United States.

Special Note: Some researchers and law enforcement officials define outlaw bikers as a form of enterprise/organized crime. The following Outlaw Bikers Strategic Assessment serves as an example of the strategic threat/risk analysis application process.

PROBLEM-SOLVING CORNER

OUTLAW BIKERS STRATEGIC ASSESSMENT

Strategic Assessment: History of Outlaw Bikers

The outlaw biker culture emerged after World War II. Former soldiers, looking for renewed excitement and adventure, turned to motorcycles and the open highways. In the early years, outlaw bikers committed a variety of criminal offenses, including public drunkenness, disorderly conduct, and murder. Some reckless behaviors were likely the result of combat experiences and traumatic stress. Establishing and maintaining the tough guy image became an obsession and violent lifestyle for these outlaw bikers.

Patches and tattoos have particular symbolic significance to outlaw motorcycle gangs. Law enforcement officers often interpret outlaw bikers' history and status from their tattooed bodies and distinguishing clothing. Tattoos with full colors require a five-year membership. Members in good standing, on departure, can keep their tattoos; however, the date they left will be tattooed. Members who are expelled from the outlaw gangs are forced to have their tattoos blemished and removed, using a red hot spoon.

Use of Force/Intimidation

Identifiable anti-establishment images and reckless criminal behaviors embraced a new generation of youthful members in the 1950s. Knifes, broken beer bottles, and chains were the early weapons of choice. Firearms later served a more contemporary version of the outlaw biker's anti-social rage. This lawless role model attracted unstable outlaw biker members who identified with the violent, intimidating, and criminal persona.

The Hell's Angels dictum is an indicator of their secrecy and violence: "Three can keep a secret if two are dead." The penalty for being an informant is death; and the strict code of silence is enforced. This subculture uses insider jargon that implies acceptance and group solidarity, for example, "jam" (courage) and "suck up to the bulls" (to talk to or act friendly to a police officer), and "a cat walk" (to drive with the front wheels of a motorcycle off the ground).

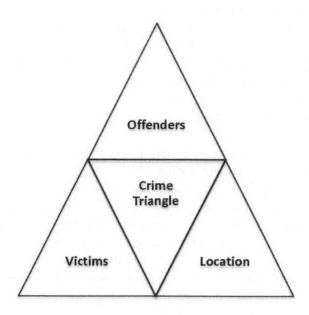

Figure 8-2. Crime Triangle

Source: Adapted from Clarke, Ronald V. and John E. Eck, Crime Analysis for Problem-Solvers: In 60 Small Steps, U. S. Department of Justice: Community Oriented Policing Services (Washington DC: GPO, 2005).

The beer, adventurous women, barroom brawls, and Harley-Davidson motorcycles appealed to a bored generation of returning warriors. They were wild rebels, breaking the law for the sheer joy of experiencing an intense adrenaline surge. Somewhere along the way from the media-portrayed youth culture world of leather jackets, chains, and tattoos, biker members transitioned to committing criminal acts for profit.

Expansionist Tendencies

The hell-raising biker clubs of the post-war era evolved into self-perpetuating, criminal organizations. The subsequent developmental turn moved in the direction of organized/enterprise crime, and transnational crime. This new era ushered in the American-based Outlaw Motorcycle Gangs (OMGs). A few members of the Hell's Angels reaped considerable financial rewards from illicit drug manufacturing and trafficking.

According to intelligence sources, the outlaw motorcycle gangs are primarily represented by four large OMG groups. The Hell's Angels, Outlaws, and Bandidos have established international chapters. Their interests: the infiltration of legitimate businesses, theft, chop shops (auto theft for parts), commercial sex, violence for hire, and unfolding criminal diversification. Pagan members have performed body guard functions for members of organized crime.

Criminal intelligence documents that United States-based operations provide a platform for interlocking criminal networks on a global level. Outlaw gangs have traditionally sold cocaine, methamphetamines, and marijuana. However, they are known to venture into any profitable criminal market; their operations include enterprise/organized crime, drugs, and weapons trafficking. Police arrests and seizures have discovered .45 caliber submachine guns, .9 semiautomatic pistols, .12 gauge double-barreled shotguns, and .357 magnum revolvers.

Lethal Violence

Additional brutal and criminal activity involvement includes: (1) contract killings and (2) violence directed at other battling motorcycle gang members. In addition, prostitution, extortion, and bribery represent further outlaw biker ventures. The intensity of these illegal operations continues to progress at an expanded rate of organizational improvement. Outlaw motorcycle gangs no longer rely on their bikes for committing criminal acts; the Internet has become the new vehicle. Opportunities abound in an arena that offers speed, coordination, organization, and concealed identities.

Interpol launched "Operation Rockers" to counteract the rapid development of outlaw motorcycle gangs. The objective: identify motorcycle gangs that engage in continuous criminal conspiracies. Interpol's National Central Bureau has the optimal potential to engage in liaison activities with law enforcement agencies concerned with outlaw motorcycle gang investigations. The potential profits, opportunities, and transnational associates envision future strategic ramifications for motorcycle gang expansion and enterprise/organized crime activities.

Criminal Prosecution: Vulnerability

Outlaw motorcycle gangs and their criminal associates became targets of criminal prosecution and imprisonment. Law enforcement agencies primarily focused on narcotics violations. The task force targeted the outlaw bikers' leadership and organizational structure, focusing on intelligence gathering and the dissemination of criminal information that dealt with the narcotics criminal conspiracy. Federal, state, and local law enforcement agencies started targeting outlaw motorcycle gangs with successful prosecution. Some outlaw motorcycle gangs were small and disorganized; other larger gangs were highly organized and ran more sophisticated criminal conspiracies.

Surveillance of clubhouse activities was helpful in gathering intelligence on biker members' associations, communications, and criminal activities. Wiretaps and controlled undercover/informant narcotics transactions provided evidence for convictions. Information gained from member informants, who turned state's evidence, provided inside information and evidence, which served as the foundation for convictions. Prosecutions under Racketeer Influenced and Corrupt Organizations Act (RICO) statutes for running a criminal enterprise apply huge criminal and civil penalties. Gang members did not recognize that being a member of a criminal organization was a crime.

Assessment Summary: Aggressive Analysis

Some law enforcement officials considered larger outlaw motorcycle gangs as emerging precursors to an organized crime problem, mirroring images of the Italian La Cosa Nostra syndicate. In summary, to fully adapt to enterprise/organized crime status, outlaw bikers fall short in four important areas: (1) leadership and organization, (2) reinvestment in legitimate businesses, (3) money laundering operations, and (4) corruption of law enforcement (missing organizational corruptor of public officials). The corruption of law enforcement officers could offer bikers a considerable advantage: protection from arrest. However, many police officers consider outlaw bikers objectionable.

PROBLEM-SOLVING CORNER: PROCESS EVALUATION

Strategic threat/risk assessments and POP operations are subject to continuous assessment and evaluation. Eck recommends: "The purpose of evaluation determines if the response(s) take place according to plan. This process evaluation assesses plan execution, procedural requirements and command accountability. Did the officers carry out the exact requirements of the plan? Impact evaluations concern whether police operations, goals, and objectives achieve the actual intended requirements? Did all remedial responses achieve the desired effect?

During the scanning phase, officers define the problem with sufficient precision to measure it properly. During the analysis phase, officers collect baseline data on the nature, and scope of the problem. Every important question addressed in the analysis phase will be significant in the assessment phase. This is because during the assessment phase, the goal will be to determine if the crime problem changed.

If the problem-solving process did not succeed as an intervention and prevention strategy to reduce the crime problem, then alternate solutions are appropriate. The crime problem may require redefining, additional analysis, and developing a new response(s). However, if the crime problem did decline considerably, it might prove valuable to replicate remedial responses to address a similar target. Assessment and evaluation phases require attention to details.

Police officers need to distinguish between an evaluation process and assessment as they coordinate the problem-solving process. Evaluation primarily determines if a specific problem declined, and if the solution was effective. On the other hand, evaluation also determines why the remedial action failed to be effective. A process evaluation involves comparing the planned response with actual results. The evaluation process reveals: (1) what happened, (2) when, (3) how, and (3) why. In the final stage, assessment occurs in the SARA problem-solving process, which serves the foundation for evaluation.

The first critical step in assessment: conduct a process evaluation. Process evaluation answers two questions: (1) Was the intervention put into place as planned; (2) How was it altered for implementation? A process evaluation focuses on resources that were employed by the response (inputs), and the activities accomplished with these resources (results), but it does not examine whether the response was effective at reducing the problem (outcomes). For that, you need an impact evaluation.

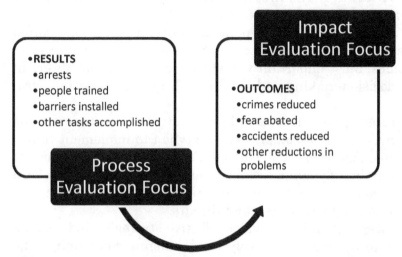

Figure 7-3. Focus of Process and Impact Evaluations (Adapted from Clarke & Eck, COPS U.S. Dept. of Justice)

In summary, did planned responses meet community needs, and a particular hot spot? Continuous reevaluation is part of the cycle and problem-solving process. An impact evaluation tells you whether the problem changed. Impact evaluations determine what happened after the implementation of the plan, including officer and citizen response(s).

Impact evaluations attempt to examine results: (1) Did the problem decline? and (2) Did the response cause the decline? Results determine if further resources, personnel power, and logistics, may serve future similar projects. Refer to Figure 7-3 for an illustration of a Process and Impact Evaluation.

Some problem areas include: (1) Plausible explanations of how the response reduces the crime problem, (2) the relationship between the present response and decline of crime problem, or the absence of the response and an increase in problem, (3) the response must precede the problem, and (4) there are no other plausible explanations."

Source: Adapted from: John E. Eck, *Assessing Responses to Problems: An Introductory Guide for Police Problem-Solvers*, U.S. Department of Justice: Community Oriented Policing Services (COPS) (Washington DC: GPO, 2002).

FOCUS POINTS

The strategic plan provides a model for police organizations to move forward. The first step: review the mission and vision statement and assess stated goals.

An excellent strategic plan examines police organization values and defines department criteria for achieving successful outcomes. Most importantly, a strategic plan guides officers in their decision-making and inspires effective changes in operations.

Strategic planning is an end-product that strives to determine what needs to be accomplished and when to implement timely solutions. Assessing a department's strategic position means operating in a dynamic social climate. Contributors arrive at a consensus regarding the identification of prominent strengths, weaknesses, opportunities, and threats.

Strategic planning provides effective strategies and permits officers to respond proactively to a changing community. The purpose: to provide guidance for continual improvement within the police organization. The plan should motivate everyone toward the department's vision.

A police strategy requires deliberately choosing a course of action to achieve the desired result. Then, police agencies are in excellent position to respond to dynamic changes, in criminal patterns. The ultimate goal: improve the quality of community life.

Strategic planning, assessment, and evaluation are central to the problem-solving and decision-making processes. The merit of prevention and intervention outcomes determine the pathway for future problem-solving efforts. Evaluation provides answers to two important questions: (1) Did the police agency arrive? (2) Where does the police agency go next?

CONCLUSION

The strategic plan brings the future into focus. New goals and objectives empower officers to pursue innovative paths to future destinations. These primary guidelines provide the framework for independent decision-making, and policing excellence. Outcome strategies provide target guidance for superior strategies, including timely arrival with limited resources.

CHAPTER 8
POSITIVE SARA PLANNING

"The identification of a problem requires first, greater clarity of what we mean by a problem. Specific meaning to this term includes: (1) a cluster of similar, related, or recurring incidents, rather than a single incident, (2) a substantive community concern, and (3) a unit of police business."

—Herman Goldstein

SARA is the applied research system for implementing the COP philosophy and POP strategies. Police leaders assess community POP strategies using the SARA planning approach. Securing accurate crime/intelligence information and analysis is the primary consideration when applying the SARA model.

The objective: to analyze a hot spot or crime cluster pattern. Then plan the correct strategies for intervention, suppression, and prevention. SARA planning provides clarity and opportunities to seize correct solutions to crime problems.

CHAPTER FOCUS

The purpose of this chapter is to discuss the SARA planning process that supports effective problem-solving. The SARA planning process is the fundamental field applied strategy in the problem-solving process. This chapter describes the need for the application of POP projects and objectives.

OVERVIEW: SARA PLANNING

POP serves as the applied planning tool for addressing causes of crime. The primary methodology remains the SARA planning process: (1) Scanning, (2) Analysis, (3) Response, and (4) Assessment. The goal: discover the underlying casual factors that motivate and support crime problem patterns. POP addresses causes rather than symptoms of crime. The SARA planning process analyzes the factual basis for criminal activity, repeat offenses and offender patterns. Refer to Figure 8-1 for an illustration of the SARA Planning Process.

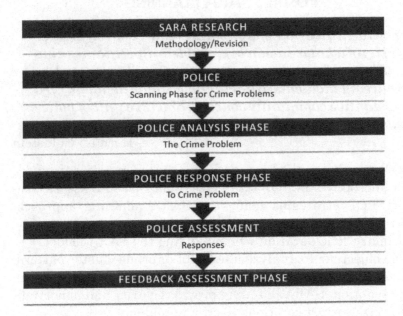

Figure: 8-1. SARA Planning and Assessments

POLICE STAR LEADERSHIP PERFORMERS

Police star performer leadership requires the application of SARA team leadership. Police teams and group leadership demand emotional self-control, self-confidence, and teamwork. Core behaviors include collaboration, and the development of officers, civilians, and citizens. Positive police leaders avoid social and emotional traps, while advancing POP and SARA planning strategies.

Positive police leadership involves applying the best emotional intelligence abilities, and connecting those skills to the SARA planning process. These leaders have the ability to focus on the problem-solving process and respond in a tactful manner. Refer to the following Newport News Police Department definition for an illustration of the SARA planning process.

PROBLEM-SOLVING CORNER: SARA PLANNING

The Newport News Police Department in Virginia appears to be an early pioneer in applying SARA planning strategies. Their police agency and researchers, collaborating with the Police Executive Forum, applied SARA research methods to their community.

Scanning Phase: Police leaders and officers identify a cluster of similar, related, or recurring incidents or offenses by reviewing criminal information. Police leaders select community crime/disorder problems among competing priorities for future targeting and solutions.

Analysis Phase: The use of several information sources helps in determining why a problem is occurring, who is responsible, who is affected, where the problem is located, when it occurs, and what form the problem takes. Analysis requires identifying patterns that explain conditions that facilitate crime or disorder problems. Information sources may include: (1) police data (CAD reporting system, arrest incident data, etc.); (2) victim and offender interviews; (3) environmental surveys; (4) officer interviews; (5) business, and resident surveys; (6) social service, and other government agency data; and (7) insurance information.

Response Phase: The execution of a tailored set of actions that address the most important findings of the problem analysis phase and focus on at least two of the following: (1) preventing future occurrences by deflecting offenders; (2) protecting likely victims; or (3) making crime locations less conducive to problem behaviors. Responses are designed to have a long-term impact on the problem and do not require a commitment of police time and resources that is not sustainable over the long term.

Assessment: Response impacts on targeted crime/disorder problems using information collected from multiple sources, both before and after the responses have been implemented.

Source: John C. Eck and William. Spelman, "Problem-Solving: Problem-Oriented Policing in Newport News" (Washington, DC: Police Executive Forum, 1987).

PROBLEM-SOLVING: FIELD ANALYSIS

A written plan that documents POP functions and organization activities should be available to officers. This plan includes the overall goals, objectives, and procedures. The plan also includes some orderly arrangement of role positions and responsibilities. Such an arrangement would result in a hierarchy of POP goals, objectives, tasks, and assessment procedures.

Police/citizen prevention partnerships can lead to productive POP solutions. Together, they collaborate and address crime and safety concerns. Effective goals and objective standards should reveal plan deviations. Remedies are applied before serious problems develop.

The following focus points serve as a review for essential SARA and coaching points:

- Begin to implement the SARA process: Scanning, Analysis, Response, and Assessment phases.
- Target the crime hot spot.
- Conduct an analysis of the crime problem.
- Define appropriate SARA response strategies for the unique problem.
- Develop proactive patrol responses in the target area.

Defining the problem requires objective analysis. Writing down the problem assists the process. Neutrality and objectivity represent common obstacles; eliminating biases is the challenge. Ultimately, the Staff Study will support the field problem-solving process with additional planning and analysis.

The next step: determine, examine, and understand both underlying and overt problem motivators. Critical insight unfolds from field interviews with police officers, and during team meetings. Encourage documentation from police officers that highlights: (1) who, (2) what, (3) why, (4) where, and (5) when factors that comprise the crime pattern. Brainstorm all possible solutions; list and describe suggestions.

Analyzing the crime triangle is a starting point for the POP and SARA planning process. Crime occurs when crime triangle opportunities emerge in sequence. The perfect storm unfolds when the offender, victim, and location, unfold with the proper timing. Crime analysts, examining essential elements, offer opportunities to engage successful prevention and law enforcement strategies. Refer to Figure 8-2 for an illustration of the Crime Triangle.

Crime opportunities multiply when capable guardians are absent. Identifying guardians, partners, stakeholders, and clients creates the social network for solving the crime triangle problem. Target hardening and security technology may offer additional crime prevention support.

POP encourages thinking "outside the box." Creative ideas about the future shape the police agency's destiny. Futuristic thinking develops effective responses to the criminal elements in a community and serves citizens well. Problem-solving requires a staff officer to research the problem, identify issues, develop and evaluate alternatives, and recommend effective solutions based on relevant facts.

The staff study can serve as a strategy to address potential futuristic community problems. In addition, the staff study generally conforms to the problem-solving model; it is both a formal military problem-solving process and a format. The staff study is then presented in written decision briefing format. The following Problem-Solving Corner discusses how the staff study forms the foundation for strategic planning, POP, and SARA future planning strategies.

PROBLEM-SOLVING CORNER: STAFF STUDY

The military provides the opportunity for proposals and innovation through the staff study. Completed staff work is presented in a logical format, which parallels police strategic planning procedures. Police officer line recommendations may move to a staff study, which is presented to police commanders, in the form of a recommendation.

The military staff study is usually a combination of written and oral presentations.

- Analyze the problem.
- Develop alternative solutions and a recommended solution. The solution format may take the form of first, second, and third choices.
- Develop the sequential and recommended steps for the solution, and execution for problem-solving.
- Present all of the related realities (political, social, economic, logistical) and other related consequences.
- The commanders (the Chief of Police, senior police leaders) may select one of the presented options or reject the proposal and recommend future research.

Preparing the Staff Study

Procedures for preparing a staff study include the following seven steps:

1. *Identify and state the problem.* This step is crucial because the actual problem may not be obvious. Therefore, before undertaking the study, the staff officer must determine exactly what the problem is and precisely define the problem's scope and limitations. The staff officer writes the problem statement as an infinitive phrase and submits it for approval to the authority directing the study. The directing authority also approves any later changes in the staff study's scope or direction.

2. *List facts and assumptions.* After completing the problem statement, the staff officer lists all facts bearing on the problem. If crucial facts are not available, the staff officer uses valid assumptions to replace facts and describe conditions. The staff officer must fulfill these requirements before accepting the conclusions without reservation.

    The staff officer states the assumption in the future or conditional tense (for example, will or might be this or that). Assumptions are grounded in factual information. They are statements that may or may not be true; however, available data indicate that they are true or will be true at some time in the future. A valid assumption would be a fact if current data could prove it.

3. *Develop possible solutions.* After listing all known facts and valid assumptions, the staff officer poses possible solutions. He may want to brainstorm possible solutions before doing intensive research. An "obviously best" solution is rare. After extensive evaluation, the staff officer selects the best available solution, screening out infeasible or unacceptable alternatives. The staff officer analyzes the remaining alternatives against previously determined evaluation criteria, using an "advantages and disadvantages" format.

4. *Research and collect data.* After developing possible solutions, the staff officer begins to collect additional corroborating facts. Primary sources of information are official documents, technical reports, manuals, previous staff studies, and resources available from libraries. The

staff officer may also find information in sources such as technical libraries, bibliographies and abstracts, and computer searches.

If time permits, and if it seems appropriate, the staff officer can supplement official data with original data from persons intimately connected with the problem, including experienced local colleagues, subject-matter experts, and operational personnel who have first-hand knowledge of the problem. Methods to consider for collecting original data might include interviews (either by telephone or personal visits), letter requests for specific information, or questionnaires administered to operational personnel.

5. *Interpret data.* As data collection progresses, the staff officer begins to prepare his list of possible solutions. They should reject all unsuitable alternatives and also identify areas of potential disagreement. Dealing with this now helps eliminate or reduce possible non-concurrences. During the research, the staff officer should ask: Is this solution: (a) Feasible? (b) Acceptable? (c) Suitable?

Feasible solutions can be implemented with available resources.

Acceptable solutions are those worth the cost or risk involved in their implementation.

Suitable solutions are those that actually solve the problem. Looking at feasibility, acceptability, and suitability will help direct further research by eliminating unsatisfactory solutions, identifying solutions, and checking them for non-concurrences. It will also call attention to the facts and evaluation criteria needed for evaluating alternative solutions.

6. *Evaluate alternative solutions.* To do the staff study properly, the staff officer must consider all reasonable alternatives (courses of action) as possible solutions. The staff officer relates the evaluation criteria to the known facts and valid assumptions. These criteria serve as the yardstick against which the staff officer measures all alternatives. Next, the staff officer compares and contrasts alternatives. The best solution will be the most feasible, suitable, and acceptable solution.

7. **Prepare the staff study.** The staff study consists of a summary sheet (body) and annexes. Along with these basic paragraphs, the summary sheet may include:

o   A list of annexes
o   Concurrences
o   Non-concurrences
o   Considerations of non-concurrences
o   A list of annexes added to summarize lengthy non-concurrences and their considerations
o   Action by the approving authority
o   An implementing support document

Annexes contain details and supporting information. The staff officer uses them to keep the summary sheet concise so that readers can use it as a ready reference. Annex A contains implementing memorandums, directives, or letters submitted for signature or approval. Other annexes contain detailed data, lengthy discussions, execution documents, and bibliographies.

Coordinating the Staff Study

Conducting staff studies normally involves coordination with other staff officers to obtain concurrences or non-concurrences on desired recommendations and other aspects of the study. The staff officer must anticipate non-concurrences. He should write considerations of non-concurrence, assess them objectively and accurately, and introduce enclosures (annexes) to the staff study.

Common Problems of Staff Studies

The following is a list of the most common problems found in staff studies. Staff officers should review this list before beginning a staff study. The officer can evaluate presentation effectiveness by answering the following questions:

o   *Is the topic too broad?*
o   *Is the problem properly defined?*
o   *Are facts or assumptions clear and valid?*
o   *Are there any unnecessary facts or assumptions?*

o   *Are there any facts that appear for the first time in the discussion?*
o   *Are there a limited number of options or courses of action?*
o   *Are evaluation criteria invalid or too limited?*
o   *Is the discussion too long?*
o   *Is the discussion incomplete; must the reader look at annexes?*
o   *Does the conclusion include a discussion?*
o   *Is the logic incorrect or incomplete; does the conclusion follow from analysis?*
o   *Can the solution be implemented within resource or time constraints?*
o   *Do the conclusions and recommendations answer the problem?*
o   *Is there an "implementing" directive?*
o   *Have new criteria been introduced?*

Source: The information contained above is adapted from the United States Army Field Manual 101-5, Staff Organization and Operations, 31 May 1997.

SCOPE OF THE PROBLEM

Law enforcement agencies interested in reducing crime build on POP crime control and prevention strategies. First, agencies establish a statement of the POP problem and needs assessment. The statement encourages police leaders, stakeholders, clients, and other decision makers to support the POP project. A current needs assessment remains an essential part of the process, which determines responses and courses of action.

The scope of the problem should describe areas of concern and the affected target or hot spot location. It should also identify the basic dimensions of the problem, define a POP project remedy, portray human needs, and avoid technical language. Subsequently, police leaders should be able to anticipate the scope of the problem, and the solution.

Determine the Statement: POP Problem

A working POP statement should follow the problem summation. Generally, police POP coordinators remain best suited to define the statement of the problem and present it at a staff study briefing. The statement of the problem serves as a transition between the problem description and related goals and objectives. In other cases, a COP and POP philosophical statement supports the hierarchy of goals and objectives.

POP Narrative Description

The narrative description includes the POP mission, police department goals, and POP objectives. Performance indicators measure the POP project's stated achievement criteria. In brief, the stated POP objectives are measurable and clearly defined. Can achievement be verified in some measurable way?

Listed below are standard ways of writing objectives:

- The POP objective description should be specific, concise, and short. The statement should contain an action verb and measurable criteria. This avoids multiple interpretations, reader confusion, and misapplication.
- Avoid police jargon and unnecessary acronyms that inhibit reader understanding.
- Design POP objectives that are challenging; however, attainable and controllable. Police teams will not pursue objectives that are unattainable.
- Identify all related objectives that are essential to the POP project. For example, internal police administrative objectives, tactical objectives, and community objectives may have interconnected and coordinated outcomes.
- Coordination with clients, patrons, and supporters encourages arriving at a mutual consensus concerning the objectives, and stated values of the police agency. Resistance to some objectives should be anticipated; some accommodation is generally necessary.

Making the POP project SMART helps avoid resistance:

- **S**pecific: Define POP project objectives with precision that avoids misinterpretation.
- **M**easurable: Define POP performance indicators or measurement criteria.
- **A**ggressive: Design and write challenging POP objectives that motivate officers to exceed their grasp.

- **R**ealistic: Place POP objectives within reach of officers, and their teams.
- **T**iming: Specify timelines, milestone measurements, and suspense dates, to achieve the stated POP objectives.

Define Goals and Objectives

Targeted goals should come from the statement of the problem. Goals are measurable, broad statements, directed toward outcomes. They point the general direction, and provide guidance for others to follow. The goals statement ultimately serves as the foundation for written immediate and intermediate objectives and could include actions to:

- Apply nontraditional methods of crime prevention
- Reduce the actual level of crime
- Minimize the perceived fear of crime
- Analyze crime generators
- Evaluate goals and related objectives for efficiency and effectiveness

Write Related Objectives

Police leaders determine specific POP objectives after formulating a philosophical statement and general goals. POP objectives measure and constitute specific tasks, conditions, and standards for assessment. They also should be precise and specific, defining target(s), times, and specific baseline outcomes.

Formulate Responses

After the pre-assessment and scanning phase, police leaders collaborate with stakeholders and community members to formulate traditional and nontraditional remedial responses. Responses may vary according to targets, offenders, victims, and cluster of crimes. Crime analysis and statistical analysis are at the core of problem-oriented policing and the SARA planning process.

Develop Plans

Working plans identify steps and procedures necessary for the accomplishment of goals and objectives. Plans should remain specific, yet flexible, and identify terms, steps, and procedures. Once developed, managers assign working plans to individual teams or officers.

During this phase, leadership and motivational factors begin to influence productivity. Work plans should include numerous POP tasks; for example, conducting a preliminary study in the hot spot or target zone. In addition, locations and who supervises the administering of the first pre-assessment opinion survey is prescribed. The pre-assessment survey includes both the target and control group areas.

Crime analysts should gather and assess the data and develop remedial POP action plans. Within one year after the initial survey, they should (1) administer a follow-up study to check progress and (2) analyze the response phase remedial actions and treatments in the target and control group areas. Next, they should compare and contrast citizen results with pre- and post-assessment surveys to determine whether improvements concerning crime prevention and public opinion have changed.

WRITING POP OBJECTIVES

Objectives identify who will implement the desired POP tasks, which must be reasonable and attainable. Objectives motivate and inspire each officer toward a higher degree of proficiency.

Objectives are not impossible and have a reasonable opportunity for logical and successful outcomes:

- Does the POP objective make sense?
- Does the POP objective synchronize with other police goals?
- Do POP goals and objectives have operational or policing risks?
- Do officers have the knowledge, skill, and resources to accomplish POP objectives?

POP Project: POP Action Plan

POP project planning and excellent performance require dividing the project into manageable segments. This means describing necessary work tasks that lead to project completion. The logistical description serves as the basis for scheduling and resources planning. Define police and civilian roles and responsibilities. Task team members and describe personnel requirements.

Develop mission orders that inform officers regarding tasks and POP project requirements. The mission order explains what should be done, but not how to do it. The "how to" is left to involved officers in the POP project. Objectives must have a specific task, condition, and standard. Conditions are forces that officers operate under in the field. The standard allows for the proper evaluation of the task. The objective must be specific and measurable. Note the following example and illustration:

Task 1: Police Teams in "C" sector will conduct frequent checks of Automated Teller Machine (ATM) locations.

Condition: Police teams will respond to ATM locations whenever patrol units are not responding to calls for service.

Purpose: The objective is the prevention of ATM robberies and protection of citizens making transactions in sector "C."

Standard: The objective is for POP teams to reduce ATM robberies by 50 percent.

POP Project Work Plan

Work plans are specific but flexible, and they identify POP teams, steps, and procedures necessary to accomplish objectives. Once the sergeant develops work plans, officers are assigned to POP individual teams or officers. At this point, leadership and motivational factors begin to influence POP productivity.

Work Plan Example

- Adopt the POP approach to cultivate and train citizens to recognize ATM crime prevention issues.
- Develop a citizen's robbery training curriculum that addresses the level of crime and fear of crime in that community. Implement the following POP project strategies:

(1) crime analysis of the ATM locations, (2) gain the cooperation of patrons, clients and citizens, (3) develop citizen
education programs, and (4) administer crime prevention
surveys.
*   Distribute pertinent information and other relevant data to
    each Neighborhood Watch Program. Organize the com-
    munity and instruct in crime prevention techniques, that
    is, ATM target hardening, and so on.

POP NETWORK DIAGRAM

The work plan network diagram illustrates and tracks the
amount of time to complete the POP project. This work network
diagram describes the timing sequence and estimates the time
factor for each POP supporting activity. Moreover, the network
diagram is a flow chart that illustrates the sequencing of POP
project activities.

The purpose of the POP network diagram: plan and rehearse
different strategies before executing performance activities and
related tasks. Network diagrams include three basic POP components: (1) milestones, (2) activities, and (3) time duration. Time
study duration factors link activities, and the successful POP
acquisition of milestone events.

Milestone events are recorded accomplishments in the pathway of the POP project. The achievement of milestone events
measures progress toward the successful resolution of the POP
project. Milestone events typically measure the beginning,
middle, or end of the project. In addition, milestone events may
indicate other significant lead-up activities, which push POP
projects to completion.

The basic units of work performed during the POP project
identify significant activities. For example, the POP project activity (work unit) starts with the scanning phase to identify the
causes of the crime problem. This will require a citizen pre-
assessment survey; the completion of this activity will lead to a
milestone. The survey identifies time duration analysis and officers necessary to complete the activity. The completion of the
pre-assessment survey constitutes the accomplishment of a
milestone.

The duration, or time factor, consists of the total number of
work hours or weeks necessary during activity. The temporal or

time factors include the quantity of work effort to accomplish the particular activity. In addition, activity planning includes locating available personnel or officers necessary to perform the activity. The identification of officers and civilians that have the necessary skills to perform and achieve activity completion is part of the planning process.

The units of time that define duration represent the number of work periods required to complete the POP activity. Work effort is the amount of time an officer or civilian needs to work full-time on the POP activity, to complete the related tasks. For example, it may require three officers working for one week (40 hours) to complete the citizen pre-assessment survey in the scanning phase. Refer to Figure 8-3 for an illustration of a Work/Network Diagram.

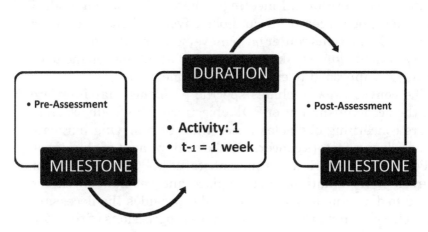

Figure 8-3. Network Diagram

In summary, the network diagram estimates the time duration, activities, and milestones for successful accomplishment. Recording work planning data assures logical progressions and flow chart analysis. The charting process is easy to follow with organized symbols. For example, refer to Figure 8-3: Network Diagram boxes with the letter "t" for time, duration, for example, "1" equals one week (t1), and the arrows indicate the direction or flow of work. Once an activity reaches conclusion, the next arrow indicates milestone achievement. Arrows drive the work diagram flow chart to the next POP activity. Then record the milestone, which leads to the next POP activity destination.

POP PROJECT APPRAISALS

The problem-solving process may offer several proactive outcomes: (1) eliminating the problem, (2) reducing the repeated occurrence or offense, (3) reducing the number of injuries related to criminal offenses, (4) improving the police procedures for handling the crime or citizen problem, and (5) altering the environmental factors, social fabric, and environmental design issues, that contribute to the crime problem.

The POP appraisal is a formal process for setting objectives, and measuring their advancement. The POP appraisal offers a well-thought-out approach that provides opportunities to assess officer performance. If implemented correctly, appraisals have the potential to improve positive POP objective outcomes.

Appraisals are formal meetings where the officer and shift commander, or sergeant, discuss objectives and the evaluation progress. Discussions center on achievements related to POP objectives or inadequate task performance. The discussion includes a forthright approach to each POP team member.

The conversation includes specific problems that interfere with the accomplishment of POP objectives. The feedback from officers concerning obstacles is essential to removing barriers. Discuss elusive factors concerning the achievement of objectives.

Police leaders review the current status of POP objectives for progress or termination, then, replace and set new objectives related to department goals. The leader provides the necessary feedback concerning the need for future progressions of the POP planning process.

Police leaders consult with police team officers to verify if the crime problem still exists. Key Question: Is the crime problem resolved? If not, conduct an after-action briefing and acknowledge lessons learned. What kind of action can be taken to improve or eliminate the problem? This requires going back to the original solution and finding new strategies to resolve the crime problem.

FOCUS POINTS

The commander's staff presents three best solutions in a visual or computer format. Then the problem-solving decision is implemented according to staff consensus; however, the commander or chief executive makes the final choice. A military staff study format applies well to strategic planning and problem-solving policing.

The military staff format recommends the following:

- *Identify and state the problem.*
- *List the facts and assumptions.*
- *Develop possible solutions.*
- *Research and collect the data.*
- *Interpret the data.*
- *Evaluate alternative solutions.*

Police leaders and their officers find direction and success when POP objectives are stated. Then, officers understand the importance of achieving the stated outcomes. Moreover, officers can anticipate how to best position their response(s), and where they can contribute to the police mission.

Objectives cascade down the chain of command to each sector and beat. Overall goals are visualized by officers, directing them to seize the objectives.

The police department depends on a team effort that is supported by each individual officer. Operation orders that originate from command down to captains, lieutenants, and sergeants, improve performance and the execution of POP objectives.

Any breakdown of a specific objective, that addresses a POP project target, is linked to performance indicators. Police leaders determine objectives that need to be achieved in advance of specific dates. Officers are tasked to accomplish specific objectives that their leaders consider necessary for project success.

Police leaders describe what their officers must do, and determine performance levels required to achieve objectives. Officers and civilians must be able to connect the dots to POP objectives.

Select the best POP solution, and praise officers for their participation. Then, forward conclusions/solutions up the chain of command. In response, the staff puts the action plan together, and implements the best solution. Provide the necessary feedback to police field teams.

Excellent SARA research methods for designing and implementing appropriate surveys require patience. Agencies must follow the correct requirements to ensure reliability and validity.

Excellent research justifies POP positive or negative outcomes and financial expenditures.

CONCLUSION

The process of determining SARA objectives is important. SARA should not be restricted to short-term objectives; the emphasis is also on addressing long-term underlying crime and related circumstances. SARA planning has the potential to impact crime strategically, as well as tactically.

Officers must be motivated to accomplish objectives, the appraisal process assists in measuring motivation. The ownership for objective success and positive outcomes is earned in POP team discussions, and the feedback process. SARA planning presents a great strategic opportunity to explain the importance of certain targets, their feasibility, acquisition, and implications.

CHAPTER 9
POSITIVE PROBLEM-SOLVING: POP PROJECTS

"The first step in problem-solving policing is to move beyond just handling incidents. It calls for recognizing that incidents are often merely overt symptoms of problems. This pushes the police on two directions: (1) It requires that they recognize the relationships between incidents (similarities of behavior, location, persons involved, etc.); and (2) it requires that they take a more in-depth interest in incidents by acquainting themselves with some of the conditions and factors that give rise to them."

— Herman Goldstein

Community and neighborhood crimes can produce a climate of fear. Positive leadership and policing not only concern the level of crime; they also address the fear of crime. POP strategies require examining underlying crime generators that increase both the level and fear of crime. The successful resolutions of crime-related problems are contingent on targeting similar offenses and crime analysis.

POP projects represent basic police management mechanisms to address a variety of community needs. Police projects begin with ideas about improving community crime prevention and law enforcement. POP projects foster sharing timely information with appropriate community members, concerning crime hot spots and crime generators. These projects target criminal activities and appraise contributory causes of crime.

CHAPTER FOCUS

Problem-solving skills require identifying audiences, and those who will have input concerning a POP project. This chapter addresses POP project management techniques that serve as the foundation for negotiating successful POP project outcomes.

OVERVIEW: POP PROJECT

A crime problem can be generated by the physical environment, or economic and social conditions. These related conditions can generate one or a series of related crimes. For example, poor housing, low-rent apartment houses may attract low-income residents and the underemployed. Poor lighting may lure prostitutes, drug dealers, and armed robbers to the same locale. The related population may also include other related crime generators such as: (1) burglaries, (2) drug addicts, (3) teenage vandalism, and (4) graffiti markings.

POP emphasizes problem-solving and analytical skills that help identify crime problems. The emphasis is on continuing problems that have similar underlying circumstances, and are related to repeated offenses. The law enforcement objective: formulate remedial POP solutions to related crime and community problems. The end products consist of POP tailor-made solutions, which alleviate the crime problem. Moreover, remedial solutions resolve interconnected and underlying causes of crime.

POLICE STAR LEADERSHIP PERFORMERS

Positive police leadership supports POP projects by building police officer and citizen relationships. POP projects require creativity, imagination, and discipline. Positive police leadership and emotional intelligence (EI) encourage internal discipline and officers who follow directions. Building relationships takes time and energy.

Positive police leaders identify officer strengths, and match those abilities to designated POP objectives. Police officers originate from diverse backgrounds, offering a variety of strengths and specialized skills. Effective police leaders recognize talent and rally that potential to significant community POP problems.

Police officers who engage POP field problems need to take calculated risks. Occasionally, an officer will make a mistake that requires leader support. Positive police leaders are available for assistance, building the strengths of their officers and POP teams. Positive police leaders take care of their officers and civilians.

POP PROJECT DEFINED

The POP project is a provisional and time-limited responsibility, specifically designed to provide a police service. In addition, POP projects may involve coordination with community partners, clients, and supporters. The POP project has three basic attributes: (1) specific in scope, (2) a specific schedule, and (3) required resources. Positive outcomes necessitate: targeted schedule dates, officers/civilian personnel, and resource budgeting.

Community POP projects provide additional guidance and mentoring opportunities for police leaders. POP projects assign mission responsibilities, direction, goals, and objectives. More importantly, the POP project manager coordinates scope assignments, schedules, and required resources.

POP projects serve as the SARA planning and tactical instrument for addressing the causes of crime. Evaluation presents an educational opportunity. Clarify what will be evaluated, and include the when, where, and how of the planning process. In addition, an evaluation statement identifies who is responsible for evaluation and assessment. Evaluation will eventually lead to an assessment of POP goals and objectives. Evaluation and assessment determine the quality of outcomes.

The central themes of the POP purpose statement include: (1) identification of positive and negative assumptions, (2) projection of successful outcomes, (3) logistical and financial restrictions, (4) support systems to complete the project, and (5) POP team commitment to producing desired results.

The management process involves monitoring and controlling the POP project. The first step: plan and start the project. The second step: organize and prepare for project implementation and execution. The third step: end project activity and close the project. Refer to figure 9-1 for an illustration of POP project management format.

PROGRAMS VERSUS PROJECTS

Crime prevention programs are broadly based and have long-term goals. A crime prevention program can generate specific POP projects; however, programs are never completely disbanded. For example, crime prevention programming represents endless efforts. Several POP projects may result in crime prevention awareness, and reduce the level of certain crimes. For example, a POP crime project attempts to suppress, or eliminate, drug trafficking in an apartment complex hot spot.

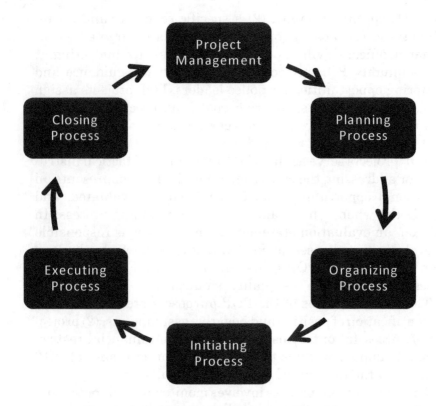

Figure 9-1. POP Project Management

POP project management requires guiding it from its foundation, through the closure stage. The initiation phase identifies crime problem needs or hot spot locations. Planning requirements detail the scope of crime patterns, time frames, and crime risks. POP project management requires communication with partners, clients, and the community.

POP PROJECT STAGES

The initial stage is best described as a general approach that includes brainstorming. The first requirement: secure a general agreement or consensus for the project need. The project manager then prepares a detailed POP project plan that meets the following requirements:

- **The preliminary stage:** establish a need for the POP project. The initial evaluation and framing of limitations are the first steps to preparing for the POP project.

   POP project documentation includes: (1) a needs estimate, (2) general estimates of required police and civilian personnel power, (3) essential timeline considerations, and (4) a preliminary list of personnel who may be involved, interested, or parties affected by POP project requirements.

- **The secondary stage:** organize, prepare, develop the POP plan, and define positive outcomes. At this stage, the plan becomes more specific and concerned with a targeted approach regarding work assignments, time management, financial costs, and other required resources. Specific outcomes include the project plan, and a supporting logistical annex plan.

- **The third stage:** establish project teams. Controlling and monitoring performance is an important factor as the POP plan unfolds. At this stage, production factors include: project progress reports, results, and other related memorandums or reports.

- **The fourth stage:** close the project and reassign officers to other assignments or responsibilities. The transition stage requires justifying expenses and closing financial accounts. In addition, this stage includes: (1) POP project results, and (2) approval from those concerned, patrons, clients, supporters, and other interested parties.

DEFINING THE PROBLEM

Defining the POP project means identifying the purpose, scope, and specifics that propose remedies. As discussed previously, the purpose or scope statement identifies the reasons and need for the project. The scope of statement addresses the tasks and conditions of the objectives and who performs the related objectives. The stated assumptions address certain and uncertain information that support the operation concept. Results, time frames, and resources are stated as limitations in the scope statement of the plan.

The first step for police agencies: identify the problem from a field perspective. The next step: eliminate blocks or obstacles to solving the problem. Every police department experiences approximately three general types of problems: (1) petty annoyances, i.e., panhandling, (2) large problems, i.e., burglary and automobile theft rings, and (3) persistent problems, i.e., organized crime drug dealing.

Analysis requires critical thinking and problem-solving for successful crime prevention and intervention strategies. Crime suppression represents an additional policing objective. Common sense and in-depth analysis, plus critical thinking, provide the foundation for appropriate responses. Analysis is a basic requirement for detecting recurring crime patterns in neighborhoods. Problem-solving infers analysis that will result in uncovering patterns and crime trends and eventually identify productive solutions.

Analysis actions are at the core of causation and problem-solving solutions. The causes of crime, and their interconnected relationships, lead to patterns for strategic and tactical applications. Detecting patterns and pattern analysis remain essential to implementing related responses.

Grouping related crime factors and underlying causations is essential to successful solutions. Identifying serial offenders and repeat offenses highlight crime patterns for analysis. The examination of underlying precipitators, social factors, and opportunities provides unique insight for proactive solutions. The discovery of essential crime analysis facts, concerning locations, offenders, and crime victims, provides unique opportunities to examine core causes, rather than crime symptoms.

The POP project and SARA planning identify positive crime remedial actions. The need for the POP project is described in-depth, along with the rationale for obtaining specified goals, objectives, and tasks. POP projects specify accessible resources and desired project outcomes. The POP project also specifies a termination date and what constitutes successful performance. POP projects emphasize the achievement of specific positive results. Refer to Figure 9-2 for an analysis of an Organizational POP Flow Chart Plan.

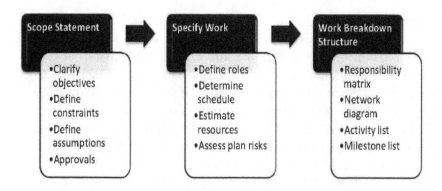

Figure 9-2. Organizational POP Flow Chart Plan

THE COORDINATION PLAN

Implementation establishes the manager, project team members, and targets the POP project plan. Tracking POP project performance documents the necessary actions to help ensure project plans have achieved proper results. Milestone results are recorded and reported.

Divide the POP project into manageable parts/phases that can be monitored during planning phases. Paying close attention to the planning minutiae, timing, and logistical resources is extremely important. Finally, measuring results ultimately leads to ending the project successfully.

Police officers may seek to expand POP project limits; this is always possible when enthusiasm runs high. Initial positive results can lead to the expansion of a pilot or POP project before its conclusion. Working within POP project limitations requires discipline. The project manager maintains control over POP project objectives.

Consult with police commanders, staff, and supporters to identify limitations. Proper coordination builds understanding and agreements that resolve conflict issues. These potential issues and conflicts are incorporated into the project plan. Staying the course demands discipline and organization.

POP PROJECT: RISK MANAGEMENT

Pop projects include the possibility of risk and uncertainty: some calculated and others unanticipated. Long and complex projects have many projected or inadvertent risk consequences. Project risk management is part of the planning process. Avoiding negative risks and taking advantage of positive consequences remains a delicate POP project balancing process.

Negative risks or threats have the potential to adversely impact reaching project objectives. For example, key personnel injured in a police pursuit traffic accident. The end result: a series of delays regarding the achievement of project objectives. Positive risks or opportunities represent beneficial opportunities for project objectives. For example, several important arrests of armed robbers reduce the frequency of ATM robberies in a jurisdiction or beat area.

Addressing negative risks requires acknowledging those possibilities in the POP project plan. Risk management means identifying the worst case scenario, and underlying problems, in the police organization and community. Risk assessment examines the possibility of risks factors that appear hidden to the casual observer.

Developing the risk management portion of the plan means envisioning and projecting adverse POP problems and their consequences. Monitoring potential risks throughout the project, as to increasing or decreasing functionality, is an important POP task. The first step toward risk management and controlling them: identify threats to the POP plan. Once one risk is identified, other POP risks may become evident.

Identifying POP project risk factors reduces adverse consequences. Risk analysis can be managed for effect and consequences. The effort should analyze specific POP negative impacts, and target adverse outcomes. There are some POP risks that can be actively managed; others are not readily available to manipulation and control.

The probability of POP risk incidence can be measured. Risk analysis examines two possible risks and distinguishes which one is likely to occur. For example, risk analysis might assess the risk or probability of an officer being assaulted during an ATM robbery, versus officer assault during a domestic violence call. Risk factors classifications may indicate: (1) high risk, (2)

medium risk, (3) and low risk. Additional forms of ordinal cate-
gorization include: (1) most likely to occur, (2) next likely to
occur, and (3) further ordinal classifications.

Decision papers offer opportunities to review and approve the
POP project. The POP project manager uses the Decision Paper
to discuss the purpose, recommendations, background, and impacts of the decision. The purpose of the discussion and approval:
coordinate staff actions. The Decision Paper should be brief and
to the point, containing essential information for the decision
maker. Review the following Problem-Solving Corner for an illustration.

PROBLEM-SOLVING CORNER: DECISION PAPER

The decision paper is returned to the originating staff officer,
or POP project manager, after staff action is completed: commander approval or disapproval, or other action by the chief of
police, or chief of staff. Appropriate processing and administrative action direct project implementation. A decision paper is
prepared in an informal memorandum format and should not
exceed two pages (excluding supporting documentation).

The paper is addressed to the person making the decision.
The staff officer or POP project manager should: (1) synthesize
facts; (2) summarize issues, and (3) present feasible alternatives.
The decision paper is prepared using the following seven para-.
graphs.

Decision Paper Details

1. Reason for **Decision**.
2. **Purpose.** A decision paper should state clearly as to what
   decision is required. The decision paper should be stated
   in the infinitive form, "To determine the ..." or "To obtain
   ..."
3. **Recommendation.** This section indicates the specific
   recommendation that the staff officer or POP project
   manager believes will solve the problem. If the purpose of
   the decision paper is to obtain a signature, the document
   requiring the signature is placed under the first lettered
   tab. If the paper presents a solution to the problem, it

includes implementation documents for approval/signature requirements.

Include the following response option under each recommendation:

Approved/Disapproved

This allows the decision maker to note the action taken on separate recommendations, by initialing the line.

4. **Background and Discussion.** This section explains the origin of the action, why the problem exists, and a summary of events in chronological order, to help put the problem in perspective, and provide an understanding of the alternatives, and recommendations.
5. **Impact.** This explains the impact on personnel, equipment, funding, environment, or stationing. State who, and to what extent, is impacted by the recommendation. If none, state "No Impact."
6. **Coordination.** All coordination is accomplished prior to submission of the decision paper. Concurrence/non-concurrence is indicated by lining through either CONCUR or NON-CONCUR, signing/initialing, and dating.

Source: The information contained above is adapted from United States Army Field Manual 101-5, Staff Organization and Operations, 31 May 1997.

POP PROJECT EXECUTION

The execution phase requires applying Decision Paper objectives. Once the Decision-Paper requirements are in place, police team tasking follows for crime prevention, or tactical operations. Project execution demands timely decision-making, and the proper logistical support.

Crime analysts provide criminal information that allows police leaders to task officers in field assignments. This form of analysis provides timely information relative to crime patterns, for the deployment of resources, and the prevention and suppression of crime.

Crime specific analysis provides support patrol deployment, special operations, and planning for specific CompStat tactical unit operations. The statistical analysis of crime patterns allows a target specific police response. Tactical planning, and the situational application of personnel power and logistics, suggests superior results.

POP project team leaders require motivational skills critical to success. POP projects move through stages of development. Expectations are high during the initial phase. Then, as difficult tasks emerge, some team members might become discouraged. Loss of momentum, due to setbacks, requires positive police leadership.

During this critical stage, the leader (project team manager) stays alert and enhances POP project momentum. The leader brings the team members together and ensures that officers maintain focus and direction. The police leader explains that every project worth accomplishing faces tough obstacles. The importance of the project is reemphasized, and the POP team is reminded of earlier successes.

Police leaders will find motivating a POP team to be one of the most difficult responsibilities. Depending on the line of authority, and POP team organization, command and control issues might emerge. Police leaders might find it difficult to manage staff and line requirements. Positive police leadership, communication, and encouragement with the POP team members can offset those limitations.

The sense of belonging to the POP team increases officer energy and motivation to succeed. The leader ensures team members understand their role, and how they contribute to the POP project. One of the best ways to avoid team disenchantment: establish benchmarks for accomplishment. The benchmark strategy provides a systematic process of comparing performance with other POP teams.

PROBLEM-SOLVING CORNER: COMPSTAT OPERATIONS

CompStat operations provide a tactical component for street crime symptoms and dealing with the fear of crime. CompStat focuses on short-term tactical operations that seek swift, targeted solutions to crime hot spots. CompStat operations require near-term and real-time crime analysis and tactical planning.

According to Rudolph W. Giuliani and Howard Safir, The Four Steps to Crime Reduction are:

- Accurate and timely intelligence
- Rapid deployment
- Effective tactics
- Relentless follow-up and assessment

Steps are carefully scrutinized; every step is required for large-scale, ongoing, crime reduction. Accurate and timely intelligence: reduce crime. What information does the Department need to know about crime?

Specifically:

- What kind of crime is happening (e.g., robberies, burglaries, etc.?)
- Where crime is happening (in what areas, and in what type of location?)
- When crime is happening (on what days, and during what hours?)
- Why crime is happening (e.g., are shootings in a drug related area?)

Rapid Deployment

Once intelligence about crime is gathered, commanders ensure that they deploy their own resources as rapidly as possible, to address crime conditions.

Resources include:

- Uniformed patrol personnel
- Plainclothes patrol personnel
- Precinct detective squad personnel

Effective Tactics

Commanders must develop clear, effective tactics to address crime conditions. These tactics must also be flexible. Commanders must be ready to change their plans when crime conditions change.

The key to effective tactics: focus specific resources on specific problems. The CompStat process provides information that enables departments to see when tactics must be developed, and track the progress of tactics when implemented.

Relentless Follow-up and Assessment

Commanders must constantly follow-up on what is being done and assess results. If results are not what they should be, something needs to change. The CompStat process is a vital tool for relentless follow-up and assessment. It allows department executives and commanders at all levels to evaluate results and change tactics and deployment based on what they see.

CompStat Summary

- Accurate and timely intelligence (What crimes are happening? When? and Why?).
- Rapid deployment (applying resources to identified crime problems quickly).
- Effective tactics (planning how to address crime, and changing plans when necessary).
- Relentless follow-up and assessment (looking at results, to make sure that plans are working).

Source: Rudolph W. Giuliani and Howard Safir. *CompStat Operations: Leadership in Action* (New York: City Police Department, 1997), 2–7.

POLICE DEPLOYMENT OPERATIONS

One common area of miscommunication: deployment operations. Patrol deployment is a level above patrol allocation and requires additional coordination. This is particularly important when officers need to be in designated locations, when not responding to calls (directed patrol). Directed patrol assignments create high profile targets and proactive incentives.

There are many variations of tactical deployments available, and innovations continue to emerge. Directed patrol provides the possibility of arrest in crime hot spots. Officers are directed to specific and predetermined targets when not responding to calls for service.

Crime analysis, directed at target hot spot locations, attempts to identify emerging modus operandi (MO) patterns. Directed patrol is the classic response to targeting hot spot areas. Special attention is given to offenders, victims, and times of offenses. When officers are not responding to calls for service, they are directed to hot spot locations. The purpose of directed patrol: select high profile targets of opportunity and direct specific patrol tactics that require crime repression, detection, and arrest.

Robberies and burglaries are open to these strategies and tactics. Police agencies have capabilities to anticipate serial criminal offenses, conduct interventions, and provide timely arrests. These crimes are not random; they present patterns for remedial responses.

Another strategy: short-time directed tactics that encourage saturation patrol, field interrogations, and targeting offenses or locations. Police leaders prefer targeted tactics because resources are in position to react to crime hot spots. Police leaders can designate police patrol priorities that may lead to apprehensions.

The split-force concept, or reserve deployment force, offers patrol flexibility to respond to tactical operations. This strategy offers greater flexibility because general patrol operations continue without disruption. This specialized response is superior to the directed patrol strategy; officers do not have double responsibilities. The sole purpose of the split-force option: conduct proactive and preventative patrol.

Police leaders deploy officers and resources for more effective targeting. Split-force options offer solutions because this reserve force is free to respond to the target without distractions. Positive leadership is the main thrust behind patrol deployments. The split-force option offers the maximum opportunity to specialize in targeting crime hot spots.

Police leaders who rearrange informal patrol operations, and attempt to manage officer patrol time, should be specific. Positive police leaders clearly explain the rationale for their direction and orders. Deployment patterns that are organized with concise objectives and specific tasks provide guidance for patrol officers.

However, leaders that overstate directions and provide too much direction can create confusion. Overstating orders can cause officers to hesitate or not comply. The individual freedom for decision-making emphasizes results, not specific methods.

When officer(s) use their own judgment and imagination, initiative leads to superior tactical mission accomplishment.

POP PROJECT EVALUATION

Evaluation and assessment is not accomplished exclusively at the conclusion of POP projects. For example, important benchmarks unfold along the way as the plan progresses. Review the preliminary data to determine the initial progress toward goals and objectives. Take advantage of this opportunity to update commanders, officers, patrons, and clients.

Initiate progress reports, reviews of preliminary crime reporting, and crime mapping results. Positive crime results inspire officers to continue to pursue the plan and remedial strategies. Preliminary reporting can: (1) highlight project commitment and effort, and (2) build trust. More importantly, tracking results can identify problems that require corrective action.

Evaluation and assessment starts at the beginning and continues throughout the implementation of the planning process. The planning process ultimately attempts to measure outcomes related to POP remedial actions.

There are four essential and basic questions:

- What are the basic expected results from the POP plan?
- Did the plan and strategies improve the crime problem?
- Have community patron and client needs been met?
- Has the quality of life improved in the community?

The second important factor involves assessment/evaluation crime statistics. Some POP projects have predictable successful outcomes, others are less quantifiable. The post-POP project evaluation ends with team recognition of project achievements, and a discussion of lessons learned, that may apply to future projects. Problem-solving requires the coordination of community resource partnerships, and stakeholders. Finally, accountability and coaching are important issues in supervising the POP problem-solving process.

FOCUS POINTS

Positive leadership focuses on officers and civilians; management focuses on police systems and procedures. Successful managers command respect when they demonstrate knowledge concerning leadership and POP project planning operations.

Police leaders must encourage effective rapport, a positive attitude, and productive social conditions. The dedicated leader understands POP policies and the community social climate.

The power to influence officers and civilians is significant in moving the POP project forward. POP managers establish effective power bases, which assist in the ability to coordinate police teams.

Maximizing power bases enhances project power; however, it necessitates coordinating influential audiences. Power bases can help energize police teams and achieve maximum cooperation and performance.

When police team members commit to the POP project, success is achievable. The POP manager's first priority: encourage each team member to commit to project accomplishment.

Concerned police leaders encourage opportunities for team members to share their commitment to achievable positive outcomes. Police leadership strives to meet professional and personal needs and strengthen commitment to POP project success.

Officers and civilians need appreciation and recognition. Police leaders can inspire officers to higher levels of performance when developing POP projects or missions that will likely succeed. Many police officers have undiscovered potential. Awakening potential is a leadership responsibility.

Effective leaders create a picture of POP goals and objectives. Secure a team commitment from each officer to the POP project. Working together as a POP team assures better success, than working in isolation. Celebrate POP team accomplishments.

The redistribution of tactical resources demands innovative POP planning strategies. Effective deployment requires target specificity concerning crime hot spots. Even short-time tactics and deployments require crime analysis and POP planning. The basic targeting requirements include: (1) locations, (2) times of offenses, and (3) the effective application of the best remedial responses.

Positive leadership that is clear and concise provides an effective operational component. Directed patrol offers an opportunity in mid-sized and smaller departments; however, it is best implemented when officers are not reacting to 911 calls.

CONCLUSION

There are many POP project challenges. Closure may take many turns, and arrival at the completion phase may involve several factors. The approval of patrons and clients is the first perquisite to arrival. Police resources affect the quality of POP programming. Lieutenants (shift or platoon commanders) and sergeants must encourage police personnel, which may require specialized patrol assignments to cope with POP neighborhood issues.

CHAPTER 10
POSITIVE COACHING: POLICE OPERATIONS

"The largest percentage of a police budget is invested in the salaries of rank-and-file police officers, and the return on that investment is largely dependent on the use these officers make of their time."
— Herman Goldstein

Police officers are essential to mission success, and police leaders cannot ignore officer influence in the problem-solving process. Line officers need their leaders' attention and support to achieve the mission, goals, and objectives. Positive police leaders seek officer feedback and cooperation. They demonstrate appropriate character, temperament, and leadership behaviors for officers to follow.

Justifying substantial financial investments in police officers, demands effective coaching, and positive police leadership. Coaching is not a single effort; it flows from positive leadership in a persistent and consistent approach. Star police performers apply supportive coaching strategies to communicate messages and maintain officer rapport. Leaders, who allocate time to the coaching process, help police teams succeed and operate independently. Coaching ultimately saves time, because it enables officers to take responsibility for their behaviors and assignments.

CHAPTER FOCUS

The purpose of Chapter 10: Coaching Police Operations is to identify coaching skills that apply to problem-solving solutions. Positive police leaders support, coach, demonstrate approval, and provide officer encouragement. In addition, a commitment to coaching can make a real contribution to successful mission accomplishment.

OVERVIEW: COACHING

Positive leadership and coaching skills drive police teams toward POP project successful outcomes. This entails definitive abilities to organize, coordinate, and support teams that work for common goals and objectives. POP managers/leaders that coach diverse teams require professional skills: (1) positively motivate officers, (2) enhance their potential, and finally (3) achieve excellent coaching outcomes. Police star performers encourage successful police team solutions.

Positive police leadership requires conflict management skills, team bonding, and teamwork. Coaching serves as the underpinning for building effective leadership and POP foundations. Moreover, coaching POP planning content areas set positive leadership themes. Coaching and POP planning skills remain essential to rapidly changing police and community responsibilities.

Coaching takes on many dimensions when assisting police officers in the journey to reach their highest potential. The process unfolds when police leaders attempt to redirect or improve performance. Positive police coaching influences throughout communication exchanges between leaders and officers. Coaching may move in both directions; officers may also coach and inform their leaders. Positive leadership dialogue can motivate and inspire police officers to achieve mutually shared goals and objectives.

POLICE STAR LEADERSHIP PERFORMERS

Police star leadership is best demonstrated in the coaching process. This is the point when emotional intelligence needs to emerge and guide the coaching exchange. The coaching content offers opportunities to be misunderstood; therefore, the positive police leader should be clear, deliberate, and focused on feedback. Coaching strategies require emotional intelligence and listening skills to communicate with officers and POP teams.

Coaching officers requires building trust, active listening, and seeking clarification. The first step: put officers at ease with the process. Positive police leaders avoid fear tactics in their quest to build professional coaching relationships. The second step: encourage officers to speak candidly, with as few leader interruptions as possible. Encourage communication that facilitates clarification and permits officers to focus on the related POP issues.

Police star leadership performers do not assume they understand the rational for substandard behavior(s). Existing circumstances can prevent police officers from executing preexisting orders or agreements. Identifying barriers or obstacles that hinder optimal performance can eliminate dysfunctional behaviors.

Appropriate coaching demonstrates that positive police leaders pay close attention. Police star performers offer constructive solutions that improve performance. More importantly, police leaders support officers throughout their attempts to implement solutions.

POSITIVE COACHING: OVERVIEW STEPS

Positive coaching and leadership provides appropriate feedback. Accurate feedback is the most essential ingredient in the POP coaching process. Professional police leaders offer information based on evidence, not speculation. Positive leadership feedback enhances dialogue when it is precise and allows officers time and opportunities to respond.

The first step: Identify behavior(s) that are counterproductive to the achievement of POP solutions. The leader reviews the officer's behaviors with objectivity.

The second step: Conduct a thorough investigation and analysis of officer behaviors that require remedial support.

Positive police leaders do not jump to conclusions; they seek valid evidence and objective problem analysis, when evaluating POP behavior(s) from many sources and directions. Do not take the word of one information source that may be predisposed to employ a biased or personal agenda.

Coaching requires collecting information that helps interpret motives or foundations that led to performance discrepancies. Does the officer know how to perform the POP tasks? Did the officer think there were other, more important, priorities? One remedy: develop coaching plans that avoid miscommunication.

The most common reason for POP project failure: officers do not fully understand related mission requirements. On many occasions, the officer will respond, "I did not know that is what you wanted." Acknowledge that miscommunication regarding performance expectations may impact a successful outcome.

The third step: A mutual agreement that existing behaviors are not in compliance with desired outcomes. The police leader encourages officer agreement on solutions and behavior changes that help solve the problem, and facilitate satisfactory performance. Furthermore, positive police leaders conduct follow-up inquiries to determine if the desired behaviors have produced positive outcomes. Finally, reward and reinforce preferred performance behaviors that achieve success and mission achievement. Refer to Figure 10-1 for an Overview of the Coaching Process.

Figure 10-1. Coaching Process Overview

COACHING APPLICATIONS

Problem-solving flexibility requires innovative thinking and self-directed behaviors. Positive outcomes emerge when officers are properly coached and motivated. Positive police leadership encourages successful performance behaviors that ultimately motivate successful outcomes. Leaders also identify and define tasks officers must accomplish to address unsatisfactory results.

Coaching police officers is an art directly related to mentoring; however, the coach must be discreet, a master of diplomacy. A low profile approach enhances communication, eliminates barriers, and increases openness. The approach may be directive at times, but usually, non-directive. The coached officer must trust the leader's judgment and experience, whose advice must be competent and concrete.

The most effective coaching method: use positive rather than negative motivators. Constructive advice can overcome barriers and improve coaching effectiveness, as in the following: "Your job performance in most areas is above average. However, if you made a few changes, you could be one of the top officers in the department. As a police officer, you have tremendous potential, and if you apply your many talents, opportunities are available. The department needs you; we must all pull together as a team."

Good coaching requires a relationship and excellent rapport. Officers may have difficulty expressing concerns about their performance, so an open-ended question rather than a specific yes or no question is often the best format. For example, you might ask, "How do you feel about your new assignment?" This is an excellent opportunity for the coach and officer to reflect on content and meaning. Coaches rephrase the question, and listen.

Positive coaching offers cooperation and assistance throughout the POP tasking process. Positive coaching offers supportive and insightful comments regarding the officer's adjustment to the POP behavior changes. Coaching also supports viable solutions to solving conflict.

Occasionally, officers engage in inappropriate behaviors, which adversely impact the mission. In some cases, the officers may not realize that a problem exists. Appropriate feedback focuses on unsatisfactory behavior(s). The first incident requires a candid leadership coaching session that specifically addresses behaviors that are causing the problem.

Coaching involves explaining standards, including how to evaluate outcomes. It may mean raising the standards, or at least teaching basic standards. Occasionally, productivity and the ability to complete essential tasks require in-depth instruction. The best coaching is impromptu. Police officers learn best when confronted with a crisis, where there is motivation to learn. Most helpful: a plan of action. Critical to this explanation is how to avoid tripwires and social landmines.

Positive police leaders communicate and coach officer expectations. They explain: (1) where (location), (2) when (time line), and (3) expectations (performance requirements). In addition, they provide feedback, evaluate and reward successes, and acknowledge individual or POP team achievements. Refer to Figure 10-2 for an illustration of Basic Coaching Process.

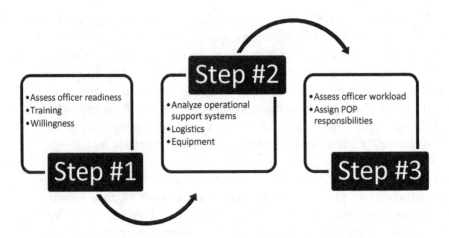

Figure 10-2. Basic Coaching Process

Defining destination, goals, objectives, and time requirements is less troublesome than achieving appropriate officer performance. Communicating dissatisfaction regarding POP mission outcomes is not sufficient. Redefining remedial and positive behaviors can motivate adjustments and heighten POP performance outcomes.

Assessment is helpful in determining what areas require modification. The coaching process starts subsequent to identifying weaknesses. The first leadership step: determine what is going wrong. Coaching strategies allow leaders to acquire essential feedback information directly from officers. At this point, information provides the foundation for coaching and learning discussions. The police leader can identify performance behaviors that require adjustment or change. Refer to Figure 10-3 for an illustration of Basic Coaching Strategies.

Some performance failures can be attributed to inadequate positive feedback opportunities. One excellent tool to improve performance: define acceptable POP solution behaviors. Specified POP standards allow officers to track and score their own performance.

Coaching feedback emphasizes POP achievements first, followed by areas of responsibility that require improvement. Offer positive police leadership encouragement and supportive POP strategies. In the future, seize opportunities to reestablish positive leadership rapport, and praise officer improvements.

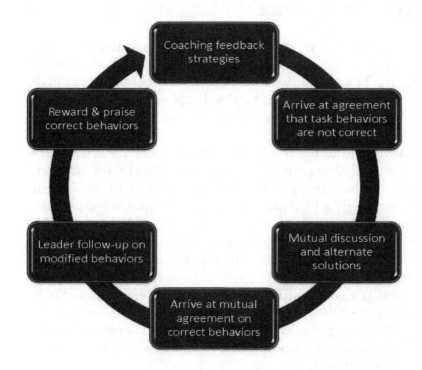

Figure 10-3. Basic Coaching Strategies

Positive leaders have conflict management skills and coaching strengths that focus on constructive leadership competencies. Zenger and Folkman apply the term "competency companions" to describe how one leadership competency can enhance another competency. In their book, *The Extraordinary Leader*, they write: "Leaders, who score in the top 10% on the differentiating behavior, also tend to score very high on the supportive behaviors. We have called these supporting behaviors 'competency companions.'"

The authors list the supportive rationale for the leadership competency related companions: (1) competency companions reinforce the related competencies, (2) achieving in one behavior helps the related behavior, and (3) developing a competency companion can change the skill level of the leader. For example, when the positive police leader has the trustworthiness factor, coaching improves. The first competency then leads to building POP teams that enhance bonding and teamwork.

POLICE OFFICER RESISTANCE

Some police officers may resent POP methods and protocols. Resistance may result when leaders request and attempt to encourage policing modification. Officers may not believe in POP principles or anticipate that POP will not work. Police leaders generally do not hear disgruntled complaints made in peer group situations.

The rationale for noncompliance emerges when police leaders are at a critical stage where discontented officers are affected. Typically, doubts emerge when leaders attempt to implement changes required for POP implementation. Failure to comply may also arise from new officers who do not understand POP and SARA strategies. Junior police officers may support senior officer opinions when encouraged to doubt the effectiveness of new policing strategies and tactics.

Generally, it is not sufficient that positive police leaders know they are right. Officers must trust that leaders are accurate in their POP assumptions. Giving "telling" orders is not sufficient. Selling officers on the concept that POP will work is the better solution to resistance.

Effective communication is possible if police leaders have open and candid relationships with officers. Officers may candidly state their lack of confidence in a particular problem-solving strategy. Police leaders listen to officer responses and feedback. A positive police leader acknowledges feedback, documents comments, and responds to questions. In addition, officers are informed that their suggestions will be forwarded up the chain of command.

Officers need to understand that their observations/recommendations may work well for them, but may create conflict for the department and other organizational requirements. Individual officers must coordinate their efforts as team members. Complex community issues require centralized planning, regardless of the quality of the idea, or strategy. Appropriate coordination prevents the disruption of police services and encourages community support.

Sometimes officers think they have a better way, but the reality is quite different. For example, a police officer develops an innovative strategy without understanding its ramifications or long-term consequences. Officer priorities must synchronize with other members of the department. For example, an officer starts an aggressive program of tactical drug stops without realizing that his/her efforts impact special drug undercover operations. Coordination deficits might compromise the Vice, Intelligence, and Organized Crime Unit's intensive strategic drug suppression program.

The solution: train officers regarding new POP mission priorities. Officers should understand that the POP Operations Order has the highest priority. Personal projects require coordination and have a lower-priority status. If officers think their priorities take precedent, leaders have to explain work priorities that lead to improved performance. Team emphasis and coordination receives special consideration from leaders and officers.

Clarify the mission and sell command and staff recommendations that seek to remedy community problems. The police supervisor or leader encourages officer trust, explains how the recommendations will work, and where similar interventions worked successfully prior to this situation. Explain that commanders and staff diligently work when shaping remedial solutions. If officers are not performing because they think the strategy is unproductive, attempt to convince them that it may take time to realize positive results from their efforts.

Police leaders should strive to reward positive POP-solving behaviors. Positive rewards encourage officer participation and increase productivity. Police leaders must praise and reward correct behaviors to ensure future replication and frequency. Police leaders may serve as the only positive reinforcement for positive POP behaviors. POP behaviors cease if police leaders do not provide rewards. Verbal support from leaders is the foundation for repeating successful POP behaviors.

Praising performance and achievements is the most effective reward. Positive rewards may increase problem-solving behaviors. Convincing officers to attempt POP strategies is accomplished through explanation, training, and gaining acceptance. Police officers need to understand that they will not serve as scapegoats for deficient successful solutions.

Problem-solving skills are vital to mentoring, coaching, and training across the law enforcement agency. Mentoring and coaching are accomplished through direct and personal interaction. A meeting between police leaders and officers, that is candid and empowering, serves as a positive alternative. Continuous contact with officers is essential to guiding the problem-solving process.

ASSIGNMENTS AND EQUITY

If asked, most police leaders would give POP assignments to officers who respond in a timely and efficient way. These police leaders assign responsibilities and tasks to officers who consistently demonstrate excellent judgment and performance. Police leaders may focus and rely on individuals who have analytical problem-solving skills and experience.

Overreliance on competent officers can lead to working some officers over their maximum capacity, exceeding their personal and professional energy. In return, other officers experience less stressful working conditions. One consequence of performing in an outstanding manner: additional difficult assignments.

Police supervisors want valuable employees to stay with the department. Police leaders need to influence officers and accomplish the work through them as a team effort. This requires that all officers perform at a satisfactory level. Positive police supervisors are aware that depending on a few officers creates the impression of favoritism and disproportionate work load.

Successful POP outcomes reflect positively on leaders. These wins require a team effort; everyone must perform. Substandard performance initiates a police leader feedback conversation. For example, the officer is not following the directed patrol order for frequent checks of prostitute locations on their beat. The feedback discussion refers to expected standard performance. The discussion and leader communication concerns the officer's response and successful task compliance for the assignment.

Police leaders who believe that certain officers cannot perform POP functions, or lack abilities, will limit their potential. These judgments produce a self-fulfilling prophesy of underachievers. Positive police leaders help officers reach their potential. Artificial beliefs about police officers can lead to unfortunate human relations outcomes. Police coaching is a viable solution to deficits in officer performance.

COACHING: SUPERVISORS

The role of first-line supervisors and police officers is different in POP policing. Coaching is a mandate for sergeants. The coaching process drives the problem-solving process and requires officers to train in POP procedures. Problem-solving officers need coaching expertise to follow-through and meet decision-making requirements.

Sergeants and officers sometimes challenge the system. Some would call them mavericks for expressing candid opinions. Defend police mavericks that are often capable of valuable insight and vision. Candid sergeants or officers once found it difficult to survive in traditional policing. However, they now experience acceptance in the POP system of policing.

These audacious officers anticipate or create opportunities to fulfill their potential, maximizing police agency and community goals. However, problem-solving and coaching tend to express contributions as a team, rather than individual successes. This officer assumes additional responsibilities. Problem-solving officers seek to work efficiently, unburdening team leaders. They endorse their leaders, especially regarding making tough decisions that are necessary to meet department mission requirements.

Positive police leaders stand-up for officers and protect them, even if it hurts the leader's career. Honest mistakes are tolerated; dishonest mistakes are not condoned. Protecting your officers requires meeting political adversity head-on and standing for something that is just and right. Police officers will not take POP project risks without the proper support.

PROBLEM SOLVING CORNER: COACHING PROCEDURES

The Police Executive Research Forum (PERF) recommended the following list of effective problem-oriented coaching procedures for sergeants. Coach your officers through the process, provide advice, help them manage their time, and help them develop work plans.

The following focus points will assist the coaching process:

- Allow officers the freedom to experiment with new approaches; however, insist on good, accurate analysis of problems. Support officers even if their tactics fail, as long as something useful evolves from the process and the tactic was well thought-out. Provide officers with examples of good problem-solving, so they know what to expect in the field.
- Know what problems officers are working on and whether the problem is real (i.e., properly understood). Know your officers' assigned areas (i.e., beats) and important citizens in them. Expect them to know such information even better than you do. Identify new resources and contacts for officers and have them investigated.
- Allow officers to make most contacts directly, and pave the way when they are having trouble getting started. Allow officers to talk with visitors, or at conferences, about their work.
- Stress cooperation, coordination, and communication within their unit and with other units. Coordinate efforts across shifts, beats, and outside units and agencies when appropriate.
- Expect officers to account for their time and activities while giving them a greater range of freedom.
- Run interference for officers to secure resources; protect them from criticism, etc.
- Protect officers from pressures within the department to revert to traditional response methods.

Monitor officer progress on work plans and make adjustments when needed; motivate them, slow them down, etc. Manage problem-solving efforts over a long period; do not allow an effort to die because competing demands for time and attention sidetrack the problem.

Source: The Police Executive Research Forum (PERF).

TEAM COACHING

Teamwork and collaboration is a worthy goal; however, it takes more effort than just calling a group of officers a team.

Police star performers are more likely to achieve a genuine POP team. Teamwork requires discipline, planning, and precise communication. The leadership, training, and practice as a team encourage team building and bonding.

Important points to consider when coaching: discrepancies between desired and actual performance. Establish realistic goals that assist officers in expanding their capabilities. The ability to achieve a commitment to change may prove difficult. Police coaches pay close attention to what is being said and feelings behind the words. In most cases, gaining commitment simply requires asking officers what they would do differently.

Stephen Covey described the "circle of influence" in his book: *The Seven Habits of Highly Effective People.* The principle is an effective coaching tool. His "circle of influence" tool is useful in focusing on where the positive police leaders should spend their time and energy. Focusing on what is important, and influencing people or events, suggests focusing on significant issues. He describes three essential decision concerns: (1) "circle of concern," (2) "circle of influence or power," and (3) "circle of focus."

The "circle of concern" is important; however, the police coach does not have control over decisions in this arena. These events or concerns distract the police coach from focusing on mission performance. These distractions may have some importance; however, the "circle of concern" can create a smokescreen, and divert attention from what the police coach can do to improve performance.

The goal: (1) move from the "circle of concern" (2) to the "circle of influence" and (3) finally, the "circle of focus." If the leader and their officers stay in the "circle of concern" too long, they feel helpless, hopeless, and disillusioned. The resulting attitude: cynicism; team members feel there is nothing they can do about the POP problem.

The "circle of influence or power" represents "the action arena" of empowerment. The "circle of power" or influence is where the police coach has influence over the course of events. The "circle of influence or power" places the spotlight on productive POP outcomes.

The positive leader is willing to listen to officers and civilians about their concerns. Then the police coach demonstrates empathy and further evaluates the POP problem or situation. After active listening, the concerned leader shifts officers from the "area of concern" to the "area of influence and power."

This is accomplished through team meetings. The meeting addresses important concerns and obstacles to accomplishing the POP objectives. The coach evaluates individual POP concerns that officers can actually control or influence.

Practice coaching on the "circle of influence," by discussing it informally with individual officers, before meeting with the POP team. The police coach encourages a discussion concerning diverse options and opinions. In addition, the police coach discusses an action plan and positive efforts officers can influence. The final step directs officers and civilians to the circle of focus. The "circle of focus" represents essential areas where police leaders and officers need to apply energy. The diligent police coach defines the "circle of focus," clarifies the POP plan, and builds team confidence.

FOCUS POINTS

Positive police leaders promote the welfare of their officers through guidance, suggestions, and encouragement. They provide a supportive approach by explaining the POP project and related problem-solving behaviors. Police leaders assist their officers in improving their performance by asking questions and suggesting POP improvement techniques.

Coaching requires active listening and being available for assistance, direction, and suggestions. Positive police leaders influence officers to modify their behaviors or performance. Coaching requires dividing the POP project into its related parts and tasks, thereby facilitating problem-solving.

Coaching requires encouraging officer growth and development. The coaching process provides the opportunity to learn from police officers and establish positive relationships. Moreover, coaching allows leader insight into officer points of view and team group dynamics.

The ability to give and receive feedback represents an essential leadership and coaching skill. Providing feedback builds officer and team skills that secure related positive outcomes. Coaching and feedback require a mutual officer and positive leadership communication process.

If inadequate officer performance feedback becomes necessary, maintain a positive coaching demeanor. Start the interview
with praise for the officer's efforts. Refer to the officer's inadequate performance indirectly; the leader admits their own
mistakes. Positive police leaders ask questions, and refrain from
making accusations.

The First Step: Establish rapport, respect, and genuineness
with the officer.

The Second Step: Require officer feedback that is specific,
and avoid unclear generalities.

The Third Step: Communicate clear expectations.

The Fourth Step: Target specific POP performance behaviors that necessitate improvement.

The positive police leader seeks to gain agreement concerning
a change to desired behaviors. Positive police coaching and feedback provide information and encourage officer discretion on how
to change unacceptable outcomes. Finally, ask the officer to summarize their plan of action to correct inadequate performance.
This positive police leadership strategy helps measure officer
commitment to change behaviors.

CONCLUSION

Positive police coaches clearly define issues before directing
officers to facilitate POP goals, objectives, and procedures. Police
coaching requires accurate feedback that provides clarification
and mutual understanding. Positive police leadership/coaching
provides affirmative feedback and descriptive correctable responses to remedy the POP problem.

Police coaches explain their reasoning and justification for
encouraging change in the officer's behaviors, to a more productive role. Coaching demonstrates leader concern about officers
and encourages mutual respect. Coaching seeks to encourage,
support, and facilitate positive police initiatives and contributions, which serve the welfare of the police agency and community.

CHAPTER 11
FINAL FOCUS POINTS: CONNECTING THE DOTS

"After a problem has been clearly defined and analyzed, one confronts the ultimate challenge in problem-oriented policing: the search for the most effective way of dealing with it."

— Herman Goldstein

Positive police leaders demonstrate selfless service and vision; they place the welfare of officers above their own interests and understand that they serve the community. Successful POP police leaders demonstrate the appropriate leadership style when they: (1) show concern for officers, (2) demonstrate dedicated service, and (3) display their vision and loyalty to their community.

This is a rapidly changing world; adjustments and new answers unfold quickly. Positive police leaders do not have all of the answers; however, having the planning process in place gives them the edge for successful POP operations. Calculated risks place the odds in favor of police agencies rather than unknown forces.

CHAPTER FOCUS

The purpose of the FINAL FOCUS POINTS is to reaffirm ten basic strategies presented in the book chapters. This chapter connects the dots to police star performer leadership skills, and provides specific applications to positive leadership and problem-solving policing.

OVERVIEW: TEN BASIC STRATEGIES

Leadership through the police prism of vision requires looking into the future. Vision clarity springs from thoughtful communication that translates vision into POP strategic outcomes. The end goal of strategic leadership and planning: forecasting the future. The goal: anticipate critical events and prevent long-term adverse consequences.

Building a problem-solving organization is best accomplished by a chief executive who is dedicated and willing to move quickly to accomplish the strategic mission. Police senior leaders must operate on multiple fronts and overcome formidable opposition.

This full-scale problem-solving campaign should be accomplished in less than a year. Reorganizing a police agency is best accomplished with rapid transition. The chief executive will need to build support systems, engage everyone in the department, and senior leadership must act quickly.

POLICE STAR LEADERSHIP PERFORMERS

Robert E. Kelley, in his book, *How to Be a Star at Work*, makes some attention-grabbing comments. According to Kelley's research: "Star leaders are made, not born. Star performers, in the workplace, use a higher percentage of their talents. Star leaders work smart and are excellent time managers. Therefore, they do their work differently, and are capable of seeing the strategic picture. Someone may be a star performer; however, that does not mean they have all the answers."

The positive police leader tries to be authentic, exceeds their grasp, and excels beyond personal expectations. Star performers recognize their strengths and take full advantage of their assets when opportunities emerge. Star leaders know their weaknesses and make every effort to improve or compensate for them. Moreover, these leaders are confident enough to surround themselves with the best POP team talent available to compensate for their weaknesses.

Positive police leaders have the strength of character to do the right thing. Then officers will trust and respect their decisions. However, sometimes doing the right thing means the leader will experience personal professional jeopardy. Star performers are willing to take calculated risks. Standing for something means placing one's self at risk and demands great courage. Positive police leaders have the emotional intelligence to meet the challenges and face adverse consequences.

Strategy One: Positive Police Pathways and Strategies

ILP and the related paradigms lead the way to effective planning and policing. Lieutenants, sergeants, and police officers provide the link to middle managers and senior leaders who coordinate POP functions. Police officers are in the best position to obtain criminal intelligence and community information that top management does not have. This information is of value to the police organization's expectations and provides opportunities to serve the strategic picture.

Intelligence/crime analysis feedback cycles support the SARA Planning process. Field intelligence and analysis feedback is recycled from police operating teams. Command and intelligence staff expertise is continuously modified based on police team experience and community feedback. Moreover, new ideas bubble up the chain of command from POP teams. The SARA analysis process serves as a general guide to neighborhood problems.

Police leaders need actionable criminal information because it is essential to making effective decisions. The intelligence needs to be timely to identify the problem and its underlying causes. Positive police leaders understand intelligence cycle requirements and how to gather information for remedial POP solutions.

Positive police leaders rely on analysts to evaluate and provide criminal information, which clarifies the POP problem. Then police leaders consider alternatives through a staff study. After the best solution is identified, leaders consider implications for remedial responses. The correct execution of the plan has all of the best criminal information in place. Refer to Figure 11-1 for a brief illustration of Synchronized Police Paradigms and Integrated Pathways.

Strategy Two: Positive Police Strategic Leadership Strategies

Designing a new vision and aligning officer goals and objectives is a worthy task. The transformation means leaving the comfortable past; however, it moves into a better future. Positive police leaders communicate and inspire the new vision possibilities. Moreover, they communicate in a manner that is compelling and convincing. When positive leaders accomplish selling the vision successfully, staff and officers will join them in achieving the mission.

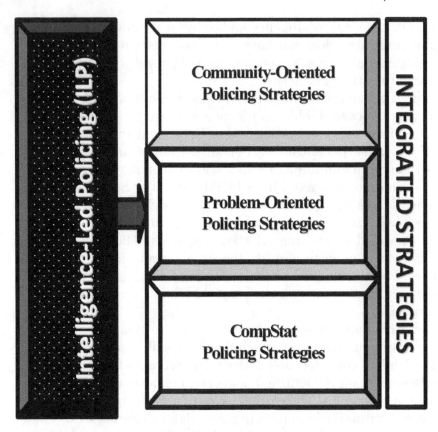

Figure 11-1. Synchronized Police Paradigms

Calculated risk factors are always part of the strategic plan and tactical applications. The speed of social change and fast-paced technology have merged and created the unidentified future. Strategic police leaders seek to convert the unknown to focused simplicity. Refer to Figure 11-2 for a brief illustration of Police Strategic Leadership Strategies.

The SARA planning model and the "Telling the Story Outline" problem-solving framework serve as excellent formats for planning and feedback. Telling the story of the problem provides the necessary outline for planning, analysis, and feedback. The most important part: a willingness to change direction and track the performance of successful benchmarks.

Telling the story remains an excellent technique for analyzing crime problems. The Staff Study allows police agencies to focus on the crime hot spot and underlying criminal circumstances. Alternatives are presented in a logical manner, which enhances superior choices.

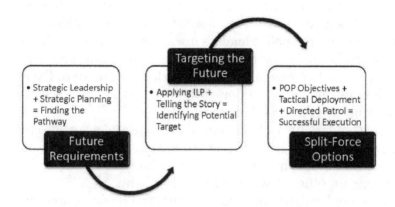

Figure 11-2. Police Strategic Leadership

Strategy Three: Positive Police Leadership: Finding the Pathway

Senior commanders influence internal and external positive and community social climate factors. Commanders want their officers to have the flexibility to achieve excellence with minimal supervision. Positive police leadership views police officers and civilians as valuable resources and encourage their many talents.

Positive leaders understand every facet of their policing responsibilities. Once police officers understand their responsibilities, successful mission accomplishment is possible. Police star leaders perform each assignment to the best of their abilities and accept full responsibility for everything that goes right or wrong.

Positive police leaders do not "go along to get along," when they know something is wrong. Going along when it is wrong has adverse long-term consequences for police problem-solving. Star police performers demonstrate courage and stand for what they believe. Having the courage to say "no" is important; ultimately, the right decision will gain respect.

Superior leaders always assume responsibility for their decisions. They have the courage to accept blame for their mistakes and accept criticism with style and character. Insightful police leaders are decisive and do not avoid a decision just because it is unpopular. Leadership is not a popularity contest; knowledgeable leaders avoid the fear of making a mistake.

Ethically oriented police leaders always keep their word. The leader's word is an important commitment. Keeping promises, even when it hurts personally, is the mark of distinction. Excellent leaders never make a promise they cannot keep, especially promises that are outside their authority.

Positive leaders have strong moral courage and are respected for their convictions. Police officers trust leaders when they keep commitments and promises. An officer, who lives by his or her word, means an officer's word is his or her bond.

Positive leaders are not obsessed with the harm others may do to them. They are more concerned about self-inflected harm. Effective police leaders admit when they are wrong. The failure to sincerely apologize for an injustice results in a serious leader self-inflicted wound.

Superior leaders demonstrate personal examples of excellent leadership for others to follow. Leadership by example necessitates working hard, demonstrating enthusiasm for the field of policing, and staying positive. Excellent leadership allows officers to rise to the example of higher standards. The benefits include setting higher standards for officers to follow and encouraging their best effort.

The police leader's responsibilities involve closing the breach between what facts are unfolding and the desired goals and objectives. Once the effective police leader discovers the problem, and what needs addressing, they must seize the moment and make the necessary corrections. Staying focused is essential to effective problem-solving leadership. Refer to Figure 11-3 for a brief illustration of Positive Police Leadership: Finding the Pathway.

Figure 11-3. Positive Police Leadership: Finding the Pathway

Strategy Four: Positive Motivational Leadership: Finding the Way

Senior leaders apply motivational leadership; they help define the way for their captains, lieutenants, sergeants, and officers. These positive leaders are not after the limelight, applause, or media attention. Their rewards are in positive leadership that ensures the success of POP projects and excellent team perform-ance. The police organizational emphasis is on shared purpose, communication, and feedback. The team must win collectively through planned actions, like team sports, not individual sports.

Police officers are more likely to respond to positive moti-vation. They respond to leaders they respect and trust. Positive police leadership relies on police management, planning, and communication skills. Leadership is concerned with motivational skills; moreover, coaching skills and a sense of humility are more important.

Positive police leaders motivate their officers by inspiring their minds to perform the mission. Leaders, who spend time mo-tivating officers, reap a positive return on their efforts. Each offi-cer has different strengths and weaknesses. Positive police leaders motivate and maximize their officers' strengths. When the leader knows and understands their officers' strengths, they capitalize on assigning the right officers, to specific POP tasks.

Personal goals are best when they merge with the police department's goals and objectives. The harmonization of the officer's personal objectives is the best method for leaders and officers, to achieve a win/win POP solution. There are higher and better ways. For example, linking officer needs to POP policing strategies. Refer to Figure 11-4 for an illustration of Maslow's Hierarchy of Human Needs and Pop Policing strategies.

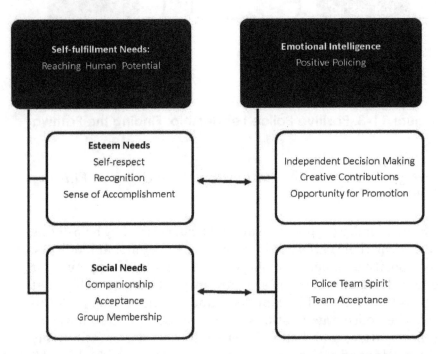

Figure 11-4. Maslow's Hierarchy and POP Policing Strategies

Strategy Five: Positive Problem-solving Communication

Communication is a two-way process that includes listening to officers. The most important part of communication: remember to listen for feedback. Inadequate information filters back as twisted logic when officers attempt to fill-in the information gaps. Misinformation results in false rumors, which might hurt police agency morale. The best formula: error on the side of providing more information rather than less information.

Successful police leaders think about the message, in advance, and plan how they are going to execute communication. Positive police leaders constantly interpret officer responses. After speaking, the leader remains quiet and listens for insight. Superior leaders are able to determine how their officers feel about the message. They are often surprised at how much they can learn about the new POP application plan.

The way police leaders communicate is important, but so is the correct channel of communication. Sometimes multiple channels of communication offer the best way to communicate the message. Personal face-to face communication is the best method; however, it takes considerable time and energy.

Emergency or crisis situations may require an Operations Order and following up with FRAG orders. Internal police communication places its emphasis on coordination with community communication primacy. Collaboration will bring more resources to the problems and accomplish added primacy than if the police agency acted alone.

Positive leadership means selling the importance of POP mission, thereby allowing officers to find the way. Leading means helping officers do what needs to be done, to change the future. Leaders assist police officers in understanding the purpose of decisions and motivate them to follow. Positive police leaders communicate successful vision requirements and outcomes.

Effective police leaders recognize individual differences and make effective use of individual talents. Police officers have unique personalities and individual communication skills. Every team member has the right to express their values and beliefs. An effective police organizational climate permits the free expression of ideas and the brain-storming approach.

Everyone's opinion is respected, as well as different personalities. Their value to the team is found in the diversity of team members. Disagreeing is the foundation for effective decision-making. However, being disagreeable will lead to counterproductive and inappropriate behaviors. Each officer's opinion is respected, regardless of their position. Refer to Figure 11-5 for brief illustration of Problem-Solving Communication.

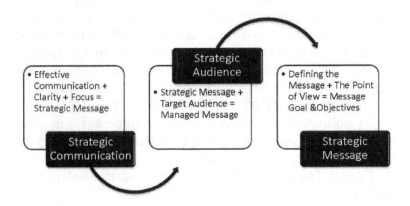

Figure 11-5. Problem-Solving Communication

Communication is a goal worth reaching for; it requires consistent and persistent feedback. This effort seeks to acquire quality interpersonal relationships. Actions communicate better than words. The positive police leader's actions will suffice. Officers must believe in the leader's ability to lead them forward. Leaders communicate the vision, allowing police officers and civilians to see the importance of compliance

Strategy Six: Positive Problem-oriented Training

The training process builds trust and respect, at every level of the police organization, regardless of rank. Training programs describe and support the destination and how to arrive on time. The positive police leader's primary responsibility: mission training to develop their officers' potential contributions. Developing police officers demands emotional intelligence and taking advantage of teachable moments. Insightful police leaders use teachable moments and instructional training to impart information to officers and civilians.

Training is an essential task at every level of the police organization; it is the gold medal of performance. The best training provides a distinct advantage at the POP execution level. Training that sets high performance objectives ensures excellent field and community benefits. The costs, time, and money demand gaining the maximum training payback. Therefore, training should match the role needs to the POP task requirements. Refer to Figure 11-6 for a brief illustration of Problem-Oriented Training.

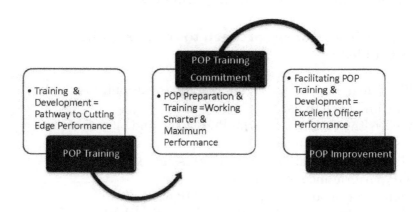

Figure 11-6. Problem-Oriented Training

Training does not necessarily require external programs that cost considerable time and related expenses. Police agencies can create internal in-service training programs that are specific to local needs and requirements. Some of the best ways to train officers: assignment rotations, especially from the field to staff, and line positions. Training and mentoring by in-service senior officers, and on-the-job training, can serve the mission well.

Strategy Seven: Positive Strategic Planning, Evaluation, and Assessment

The typical reaction to change is negative, because change threatens officer and civilian "comfort zones." Moving toward strategic change requires focusing on police department needs. Therefore, clarifying the need to change is essential to altering comfortable ways of policing. Officers and civilians must understand the need for change. Then most officers will be motivated to change their views and move in new directions.

A clearly stated POP strategic vision is decisive for effectiveness, efficiency, and success. A positive vision is powerful, attracting police and civilian support. The indisputable vision has the power to alter and inspire officers and civilians into compliance. Vision serves as a motivator to break-out of the comfort zone and accomplish the POP mission, goals, and objectives.

Strategic leaders follow major strategic premises that lead as far as the vision and increased insight will allow.

These positive leaders proceed to the next police quantum leap:

- What does the police agency seek to accomplish POP goals and objectives?
- What is the rationale for the POP goals and objectives and related accomplishments?
- What are the evaluation and assessment procedures for POP performance objectives?
- What are the potential positive POP outcomes?
- What are the potential unintended negative POP outcomes?

The first objective of the strategic plan: eliminate bias and prejudice through detached observations. Establish the methods in a POP pilot study, which eliminate future research problems.

The second objective: train police interviewers, because data collection generally requires interviewing skills. Consider independent civilian participation; this assures a civilian approach and dispassionate data observers.

The third objective: collect response data in the citizens' own words, as well as objective questionnaires. Finally, data analysis requires certain skills, in particular, statistical analysis. Hiring a specialist assists in obtaining professional research methods, accurate data, and timely results. Refer to Figure 11-7 for a brief illustration of Strategic Planning, Evaluation, and Assessment.

The police department and community win through cooperative team efforts. This does not mean that individuality is disregarded; on the contrary, individual differences and divergent points of view are important. Addressing differing points of view means that all problem facets can be evaluated.

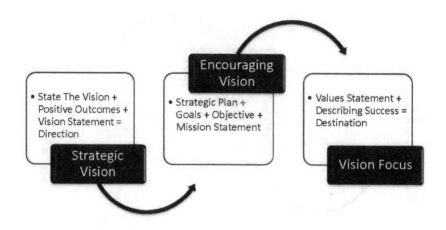

Figure 11-7. Strategic Planning, Evaluation, and Assessment

Strategy Eight: Positive SARA Planning

Commanders leave as many decisions as possible to the delegation of authority and POP team coordination. The new technique for creative POP solutions: encourage ideas up the chain of command from POP teams. Positive police leadership does not push POP team leaders to perform in a certain manner; the mission pulls them into the future.

Positive police leaders and their officers identify problem(s) by addressing them, and start by analyzing the problem. Defining a problem necessitates applying the principle of clarity. If leaders do not have an adequate definition, success is unlikely. Failure to define the problem creates consequences for the remaining SARA problem-solving process. Refer to Figure 11-8 for an illustration of the SARA Planning Steps.

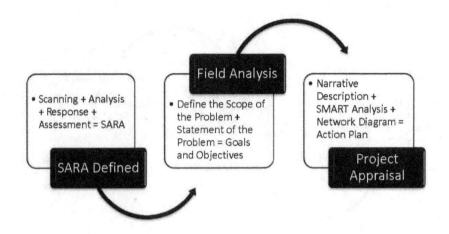

Figure 11-8. SARA Planning Steps

The First Step: Lieutenants and sergeants assess officers to determine their abilities to engage the POP problem-solving process. Dealing with underlying circumstances of crime and the public requires emotional intelligence and field experience. Problem-solving requires the combination of coaching and teaching skills.

The Second Step: Sergeants need to analyze operational support systems for successful POP problem-solving. Assessment requires examining present commitments and deployment requirements. Deployment of police units should be in response to the volume of calls for police assistance, not simply geographical boundary lines.

The Third Step: Assess officer workload and the distribution of POP responsibilities. Time studies that approximate uncommitted time factors may prove useful. Sergeants and officers can employ uncommitted time to address neighborhood issues and SARA problem-solving requirements.

The Fourth Step: Lieutenants and sergeants address police agency logistical requirements. Resources influence deployment of vehicles, equipment and POP operation sustainment. These logistical support functions are coordinated with POP teams.

Lieutenants, sergeants, and corporals, are essential in encouraging team problem-solving. Sergeants and patrol officers stand at POP ground zero for police operations. Tactical mission success and accountability depend on the sergeant's leadership, and problem-solving skills. Excellent leadership serves POP missions and effective problem-solving solutions.

Strategy Nine: Positive Problem-solving Pop Projects

Officers are motivated when the mission clarity converts to actionable POP projects. POP milestones mark the journey, and their simplicity inspires identification. POP milestone objectives attract officers to POP journey requirements. POP officer involvement demands describing what it takes to arrive on time and ensures mission commitment. Positive police leaders help plan the POP project route; moreover, they review the progress of meaningful officer and POP team contributions.

POP teams are the essence of the problem-solving strategies and an influential style of police work. This style of leadership requires the ability to plan, design, and task POP police team members. Most importantly, the successful leader efficiently delegates assignments, competently monitors progress, and motivates the desire to do extremely well.

Once police leaders have the POP destination resolved, then the correct course of action(s) might provide solutions to the POP problem. The correct solutions demand an effective POP action plan. Implementation of the plan requires communication that connects decisions to the reality of field applications. Positive police leaders define officer roles, responsibilities, and task requirements to ensure POP task effectiveness.

Establish the criteria for POP success and communicate acceptable standards. Following through necessitates monitoring progress to ensure the completion of desired POP outcomes. The effective police leader tracks project progress and takes corrective action when necessary. The goal: keep officers motivated, help maintain a positive attitude, and support officer commitment to POP project success.

Planning answers two basic questions: (1) What needs to be done? and (2) How does the department create that achievement? The desired outcomes of these objectives are tied to police agency goals. The POP team leader formulates a plan to achieve objectives: who, what, why, where, when, and how. These planning conditions involve how the POP team's accomplishments can be measured.

The First Step: Examine why the POP team exists, and how to fit the team's effort into the larger strategic picture. Community analysis offers occasions for team leaders to identify and exploit crime targets (hot spots) of opportunity. This also demands that the leader examine potential threats the team may encounter.

The Second Step: Understand the police department's goals and objectives. Aligned goals and objectives should contribute to the police mission, vision, and long-term planning. This means a complete strategic picture of how goals and objectives connect to POP action plans.

The Third Step: Implement the plan, clarify roles, and provide support and logistics. The objectives should be reachable, reasonable, and have a stretch factor for the team. Monitoring the POP plan ensures the right guidance and follow-up. Finally, determine if the results meet the stated objectives and assessment standards.

Risk acceptance is a part of finding POP solutions. Police commanders and staff studies determine if the risks are worth taking versus the benefits. POP leadership demands that police leaders do not lose sight of POP project: mission, goals, and objectives. Refer to Figure 11-9 for brief illustration of SARA/POP Problem-Solving Projects.

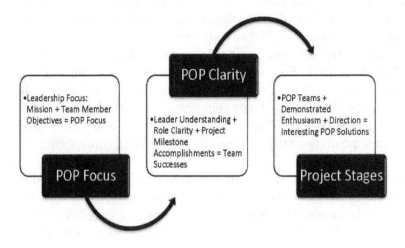

Figure 11-9. SARA/POP Projects

POP solutions to community problems require determination and dedication. Police leaders and team members must stay the course; success does not always come easily. The teams need to keep trying until they are successful; however, every POP project cannot be won on persistence alone.

Strategy Ten: Positive Coaching: Police Operations

Managing a police POP team is not an easy leadership responsibility. Police teams are composed of different personalities that present a real challenge. Gaining the cooperation of diverse team personalities is an essential leadership function. Positive police leaders understand their officers and what makes a winning team.

The teams must win interactively; otherwise, they fail collectively. Once the POP climate is set, enthusiasm becomes contagious. Police team commitment is the essential ingredient. Team members reinforce officer power and eagerness. Police officers need to feel important and understand that the POP mission is essential to positive and attainable outcomes.

POP officers need encouragement and support before they engage complex community POP problems. Problem-solving requires additional coaching and police officer coordination. Therefore, coaching time represents a significant issue for problem-solving officers.

Assessing police officers who are having problems can reduce unacceptable field performance. Sometimes officers have control over their problems, while other officers may not. The former group of officers will be easier to coach; the latter group is more problematic. The relationship between the police leader and officer is the most important component of the POP coaching process.

The first priority: establish and display positive leader regard for the officer. This essential quality assists in the mentoring and coaching process. Regardless of the circumstances, the leader should demonstrate respect for the officer. The police leader's high opinion creates a positive response, acceptance, and the feeling of being respected. This is absolutely necessary for developing the trust that is crucial in the coaching relationship.

Police leaders, who approach officers in an effort to improve performance, do so tactfully. The first fundamental requirement:

obtain the facts. The positive police leader must operate knowing the whole story, as it applies to officer performance. The need for privacy is always a primary consideration.

The approach plan should include what kind of assistance is needed to improve the situation. This plan anticipates possible reactions to the approach and basic recommendations. The police leader considers the officer's position and possible defensive reactions. The positive police leader establishes a threat-free climate that emphasizes open communication and mutual trust. Refer to Figure 11-10 for brief review of Coaching Police Operations.

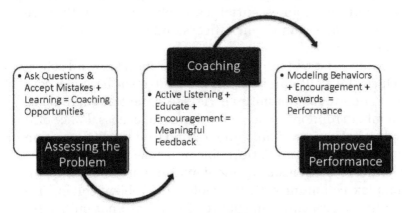

Figure 11-10. Coaching Police Operations

The First Step: Encourage an open dialogue in a non-threatening atmosphere. Start the coaching session with a positive point of past rapport. Continue the coaching session with a general discussion of problems encountered regarding the POP project. The police leader includes a discussion of the officer's past positive contributions.

The Second Step: The leader states the purpose of the coaching session. At this point, officer defenses may emerge; this is the time for the police leader to remain calm. The objective: to mutually improve POP performance; it is not a contest of wills. An additional objective: determine cause(s) of the POP problem or performance standards.

The Third Step: Assist the officer in describing the POP plan to change behaviors or level of performance. At this point, the positive police leader states the need for change and describes the correct behaviors and standards. This requires the officer to contribute feedback that indicates understanding.

The Fourth Step: Affirm confidence in the officer's abilities and improved performance. After the coaching session, the police leader follows-up to check officer performance. The objective: determine if the officer's plan to improve performance behaviors, meets mutual expectations. In summary, the positive police leader and officer might require modification of the expected plan or performance behaviors.

First-line supervisors (sergeants and corporals) provide immediate direction regarding objectives and end result measurements. Sergeants listen to team members and encourage officer feedback. They give credit for creative ideas and praise good results. Sergeants and corporals are in the best position to tell officers how important they are to the department. Successful supervisors maximize officer professional efforts under their authority.

CONCLUSION

The ultimate positive police leader destination: a sustainable future that anticipates significant events. Policing theories or paradigms are evolving rapidly; they provide protocols for timely arrival. Finding the pathway means identifying the chasm and avoiding the abyss. Once the police agency moves beyond the chasm space, it is possible to find positive pathways to the future.

The "ILP Grand Theory" provides the pathway and goals for others to follow. ILP serves as the primary coordination hub for criminal information. Intelligence analysis serves organized crime strategic investigations. Crime analysis serves street tactical operations. This chapter supports the understanding of the "ILP Grand Theory" or policing paradigms: Intelligence-Led Policing (ILP) + Community-Oriented Policing (COP) + Problem-Oriented Policing (POP) + Neighborhood-Oriented Policing (NOP) + CompStat Tactical Operations (CTO) = Police Excellence (PE).

CHAPTER 12
EPILOGUE: APPRAISE YOUR POSITIVE LEADERSHIP STYLE

"Your vision will become clear when you look in your heart. Who looks outside, dreams. Who looks inside, awakens."

— Carl G. Jung

There is something that calls positive police leaders to their career pathways and destinations. An inner announcement resounds: "This is who I am and what I must do in life." The special calling to law enforcement defines understanding and the meaning of character. A special calling is the first part of the journey; career preparation defines the true north of professional destinations. Two human relations pathways emerge and unite: (1) positive police leadership and (2) emotional intelligence.

CHAPTER FOCUS

The EPILOGUE addresses your positive police leadership style. Emotional intelligence serves as the basic foundation for positive police leadership. Police leaders can improve their emotional intelligence through study and field applications. These leaders operate in a dual framework that supports effective POP problem-solving solutions.

OVERVIEW—POSITIVE LEADERSHIP

Positive police leaders have the potential for vision because they have the ability to look within. Moreover, their self-assessment point of view allows star performers to maximize strengths, and insight into minimizing their weaknesses. Positive police leaders have the foresight to apply emotional intelligence. Effective POP problem-solving solutions focus on understanding the human component. The preceding chapters illustrated the final review points presented in the EPILOGUE.

POLICE STAR LEADERSHIP PERFORMERS

Positive police leadership encourages inspirational leadership that avoids negative consequences. The leader's journey includes arriving at a place, where positive police leadership and emotional intelligence prevail. This positive approach offers essential qualities for influencing police officers and others. Police star leadership performers target positive emotional attributes that they can apply to encourage constructive relationships.

Positive police leadership and emotional intelligence emphasize self-management as a basic requirement for implementing problem-solving solutions. Self-management depends on how the leader takes action, or presents the neutral response, avoiding negativity. Positive police leadership behaviors depend on self-awareness and self-assessment.

Positive police leadership behaviors stem from self-management and leadership competencies. Effective police leaders control their emotions; self-control serves the strategic goals and objectives well. Police leaders manage problems best by never letting others see them sweat.

Positive police leadership is of value to police leaders because it serves: "self-awareness and assessment" in the problem-solving process. In addition, this positive frame of reference allows police leaders and their officers to define: (1) what works well, (2) what needs improving, and (3) what does not work. Positive police leadership appreciates human potential, fostering the ability of officers to perform well, in the face of adversity.

Positive policing addresses how leaders can improve community problems. A positive policing emphasis is on what police leaders can do to successfully manage POP solutions. Effective police leadership helps instill qualities that improve their officers' optimal functioning. Refer to Figure 12-1 for a visual illustration of Positive Police Leadership Attributes.

Positive police leadership has applications for Neighborhood Watch, the community, and nation. This approach focuses on developing social and institutional relationships, which improve police problem-solving solutions. Most importantly, it creates opportunities for police enhancement of civic support and citizen cooperation. Positive leadership can lead to police investigations, which support cooperation with other community services and improve coordination of citizen services.

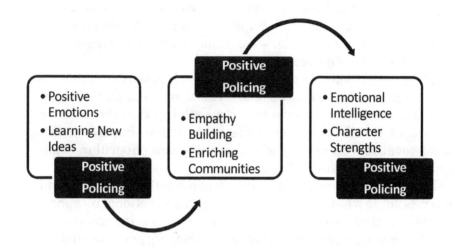

Figure 12-1. Positive Police Leadership Attributes

Source: Adapted from Bradberry & Greaves (2009), Gherniss & Goleman (2001), and Nadler (2011).

Insightful police leadership encourages basic personality traits that define character strengths. Police leaders that demonstrate personal courage, persistence, honesty and wisdom, maximize potential. Excellent character traits focus on optimal performance, and the search for police excellence. The analysis of emotional intelligence provides one pathway to achieving those resources.

APPRAISE YOUR LEADERSHIP STYLE: EMOTIONAL INTELLIGENCE

Why is emotional intelligence a necessary component of police positive leadership and POP operations? The answer is found in the related social and interaction requirements of POP policing. According to Chernis and Goleman, the definition of emotional intelligence requires demonstrating an effective balance of personal and social competencies: (1) Self-Awareness (Understanding of Yourself), (2) Self-Management (Managing Yourself), (3) Social Awareness (Understanding Others), and (4) Relationship Management (Managing Others).

Self-Awareness

Self-awareness is the police leader's ability to have insight into their emotions and manage their own self-assessment. Anticipating reactions to given emotional challenges, or situations, represents a basic police leadership requirement. Understanding the range of the police leader's emotions requires looking within at what triggers negative emotions.

The positive police leader encourages self-assessment and reflection on how and when negative emotions emerge. Spending time in this endeavor prevents the possibility that the positive police leader will take some regrettable action. Positive police leaders evaluate accurately when someone or a particular situation triggers an emotional reaction.

Emotional self-awareness requires constantly monitoring and understanding what triggers an uncalculated emotional response. Developing these emotional skills does not require going deep into the unconscious mind. However, developing personal and social competencies emerge from understanding the police leader's accurate personal assessment and self-awareness.

Star performers have insight into how their emotions affect themselves, others, and police performance. Accurate self-assessment requires that positive police leaders develop the ability to identify personal strengths and inadequacies. More importantly, how to improve insight concerning weaknesses is the best self-assessment ability. Refer to Figure 12-2 for a visual illustration of Self-Awareness.

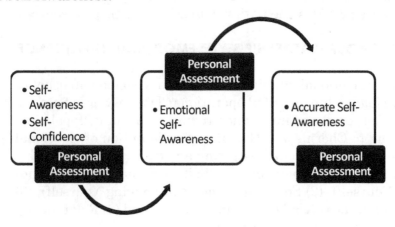

Figure 12-2. Self-Awareness

Source: Adapted from Bradberry & Greaves (2009), Gherniss & Goleman (2001), and Nadler (2011).

Social Awareness

Social awareness requires a personal assessment of empathy skills, which includes respect for officer opinions. Empathy implies understanding an officer's perspective; it is not about sympathy or feeling like someone. Social awareness requires openness and the ability to connect to diverse opinions.

Organizational awareness concerns understanding informal and formal organizational components. The more difficult part for police leaders: staying open to the officers' informal network and power structure. The chain of command structure is not always absolute and is subject to rapid change. Informal politics may have dominance over the formal chain of command. Positive police leaders recognize and account for informal or hidden elements of communication.

The POP service orientation is proactive-oriented and strives for optimal citizen satisfaction. POP and SARA solutions require social awareness and insight into community problems. Unique COP and POP strategies generate a positive service orientation that serves the community and its citizens. Refer to Figure 12-3 for a visual illustration of Social Awareness.

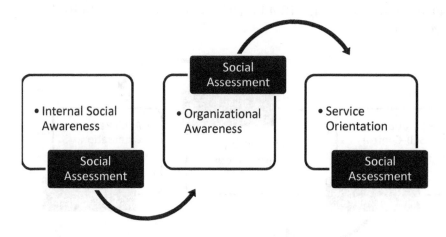

Figure 12-3. Social Awareness

Source: Adapted from Bradberry & Greaves (2009), Gherniss & Goleman (2001), and Nadler (2011)

Self-Management

Positive police leaders master self-control so they may have influence over the course of events. These leaders benefit because of their trustworthiness and, therefore, they earn mutual respect. Excellent police leaders are not arrogant; they candidly admit their mistakes and apologize appropriately.

Effective leaders are adaptable to emotional situations, respond well to uncertainty, and manage rapidly unfolding crisis situations effectively. Positive police leaders estimate the situation in a neutral and detached manner. These police leaders are able to tolerate doubt, avoid paralyzing fear, and explore available options. They operate in a comfort zone, which allows them to defer unproductive emotional reactions. Positive police leaders anticipate when the best course of action will unfold and initiate appropriate solutions.

Positive police leaders are conscientious, persistent, and consistent. They take their personal responsibilities seriously and assure that the goals and related objectives are successfully performed. Successful police leaders seize the initiative and are mission-oriented. Their achievement orientation eliminates obstacles, takes reasonable risks, and identifies pathways to the future. Refer to Figure 12-4 for a visual illustration of Self-Management.

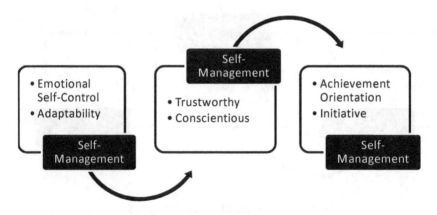

Figure 12-4. Self-Management

Source: Adapted from Bradberry & Greaves (2009), Gherniss & Goleman (2001), and Nadler (2011).

According to Daniel Goleman, self-control means avoiding having the police leader's mind emotionally hijacked by others. This is a basic component of social adjustment and developing an awareness of self, and those who engage in these behaviors. Some officers and citizens invite police leaders on a roller coaster ride at every opportunity. Positive police leaders learn how to avoid getting on emotional rides that may lead to personal disaster.

Anger leads to the leader losing self-control, and can result in many adverse consequences. Positive police leaders understand how to apply their emotional intelligence, and avoid allowing officers and civilians to push their emotional buttons. The national news media covers these emotional tantrums daily, emotional intelligence avoids self-destruction.

Relationship Management

Excellent vision and positive police leadership inspire officers to follow the primary pathway. This form of leadership direction communicates a compelling vision and POP mission. The POP mission is practical and appeals to a social network of influential patrons, clients, and citizens. However, the most influential audience remains police officers: that effort requires selling and participating.

Positive police leadership leads the charge and serves as a primary change agent. The effort requires highlighting new POP initiatives and developing innovative strategies. Effective communication of initiatives demands openness, persistent dialogue, and flexibility concerning diverse community opinions.

The spirit of success is in developing police officers, because they are on the frontlines of the POP enterprise. The coaching process is core: give timely advice, guidance, and constructive feedback. The coaching process encourages a bonding process among officers, patrons, clients, and citizens.

Positive police leaders visualize successful outcomes. The POP social network assists in developing meaningful solutions and support. Teamwork, conflict management, and partnerships, form the basis of an active commitment to effective POP solutions. Refer to Figure 12-5 for an illustration of Relationship Management.

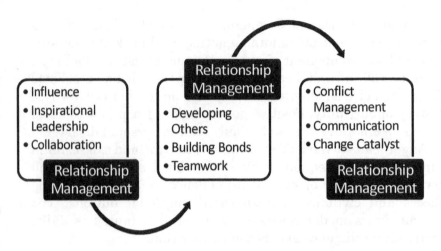

Figure 12-5. Relationship Management

Source: Adapted from Goleman (1995), Gherniss & Goleman (2001), and Nadler (2011).

APPRAISE YOUR LEADERSHIP: POSITIVE TEAMWORK

Tom Rath and Barry Conchie, in their book, *Strengths Based Leadership*, describe four leadership domains: (1) strategic thinking, (2) relationship building, (3) influencing, and (4) executing. They conclude based on a Gallup Poll: "Instead of one dominant leader who tries to do everything, or individuals who have similar strengths, contributions from all four domains lead to a strong and cohesive team." In summary, "Although individuals need not be well-rounded, teams should be."

Many police agencies advocate teamwork; however, it is not easily achieved. Police teamwork develops over time, not merely by assignment. The bonding and trust build while facing adversity and believing in each team member's abilities to achieve. Teamwork functionality demands on discipline, planning, and practicing as a team unit. The positive regard of police officers and citizens advances team spirit.

Positive police leadership requires teamwork and collaboration. Building the police climate requires candid, friendly, and cooperative team members. The development of esprit de corps pulls police team members into participation and cooperation. Positive police leaders supervise and coordinate training, and practice sessions, to achieve team-building requirements.

Some helpful positive leadership points may include: (1) praise team members when they demonstrate the right behaviors; (2) be careful that a specific team member does claim credit for a total team effort; (3) share the success of other officers; (4) demonstrate enthusiasm for the project; involve the whole team; and (5) try to make the POP project interesting and enjoyable.

Team meetings are frequent; attendance builds opportunities to communicate and bond team members. These learning experiences for teamwork include brainstorming POP strategic goals, objectives, and operations. Meetings and field encounters over a three-month period represent valuable ways for police officers to learn and bond together. Team meetings provide detailed POP feedback information and opportunities to evaluate POP project benchmark accomplishments.

APPRAISE YOUR LEADERSHIP STYLE: POSITIVE MOTIVATION

The central theme of police leadership concerns the motivational factors of police officers, patrons, clients, and citizens. The synchronization of these motivational requirements takes effort and timing. Social awareness and timing are essential for successful POP motivational requirements. Correct timing requires asking the right questions, during the correct time frame, with the total audience in mind.

The right mindset for motivation to accomplish a series of tasks includes two types of motivation. The first type of motivation is external or extrinsic motivation; the second type of motivation is internal or intrinsic. Extrinsic motivation involves external rewards: status, money, and praise. Intrinsic motivation occurs when police officers engage in behaviors for their own intrinsic value, regardless of any rewards.

Intrinsic motivation does not require rewards. Certainly, this intrinsic behavior is the ideal response; however, positive police leaders can provide only the best social climate to nurture intrinsic motivation. Police officers who are intrinsically motivated demonstrate superior performance and excel at POP creative solutions.

Richard Ryan and Edward Deci's research indicates that intrinsically motivated individuals demonstrate enhanced performance, a sense of persistence, self-esteem, and vitality. These individuals excel better than those motivated by external rewards. Their research indicated that this difference prevailed even when the two groups studied are of equal competence and performing the same task.

Richard Ryan and Edward Deci comment:

> *"Perhaps no single phenomena reflects the positive potential of human nature as much as intrinsic motivation, [or] the inherent tendency to seek out novelty, and challenges, to extend and exercise one's capacities, to explore, and learn ... Intrinsically motivated behavior is often an attempt to meet our innate needs for competence, relatedness, or autonym."*

When officers and civilians are motivated by internal values, everyone benefits. Intrinsic motivation is the ideal mindset and offers an excellent human response and intuitiveness. However, intrinsic motivation is not the most common police officer response.

Why are external rewards important? The majority of police officers are concerned with external or extrinsic rewards. Officers may not be concerned with intrinsic rewards immediately, or never pursue that approach. As cited previously, officers may be more concerned with Herzberg's theory of motivators and hygiene factors. His research overlaps intrinsic motivation with the "work itself" and "personal growth" components. However, there are many distractions along the way. Refer to Figure 12-6 for a revisit to Herzberg's Theory of Motivators.

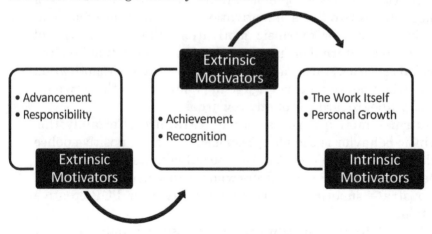

Figure 12-6. Herzberg's Theory of Motivators

Source: Adapted from Herzberg's Motivators.

APPRAISE YOUR LEADERSHIP STYLE: EMOTIONAL INTELLIGENCE FRAMEWORK

Benjamin Franklin once commented ... *"There are three things extremely hard: steel, a diamond, and to know one's self."*

Self-assessment procedures provide some insight as to what police positive leaders need to understand about themselves. However, this requires some introspection and self-criticism. This is no easy task because it means total personal honesty; however, the effort is worth the positive results.

Self-candor opens the door for becoming a star performer. Opening the door to the unknown is the best way to engage the future, and achieve self-understanding. Personal insight provides the means for understanding the pathway to star performance and professional contributions. Refer to Figure 12-7 for an illustration of Goleman's Emotional Competence Framework.

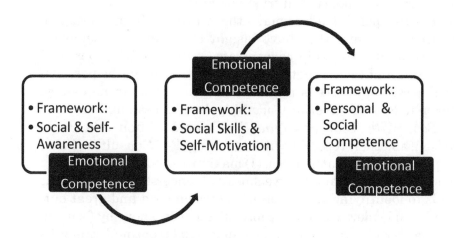

Figure 12-7. Emotional Competence Framework

Source: Adapted from Daniel Goleman, Emotional Intelligence: Why It Can Matter More Than IQ, 1995.

Positive police leaders are star performers, not because they receive public acclaim; but because they shine the spotlight on their officers' accomplishments. Positive police leaders operate as shared facilitators of POP successful solutions; they do not seek the limelight. Positive police leaders are humble; they SWOT themselves. As described previously and applied to police organizations, the acronym SWOT stands for analyzing **S**trengths, **W**eaknesses, **O**pportunities, and **T**hreats.

APPRAISE YOUR LEADERSHIP STYLE: POLICE STAR LEADERSHIP PERFORMANCE

Identifying personal strengths requires introspection; identifying character qualities in others, demands social awareness. This means taking the time to appraise the situation, and identify the potential talent in others. Positive police leaders recognize that their emotions can influence POP team performance objectives.

Positive police leaders avoid conflict with their officers, civilians, and citizens. They do not fight battles on multiple fronts and prefer win/win solutions. This form of leadership plans for an extensive network of personal relationships. The emphasis is on: collaboration, rapport, and trustworthiness.

Positive police leaders make the transition from average to greatness, because they have insight into their own behavior. This style of leadership concentrates on maximizing personal strengths and the strengths of others. Focusing on the personal weaknesses of others is minimal, and on self when necessary. The mandate for superior leadership: build on strengths.

Soar With Your Strengths, by Donald Clifton and Paula Nelson, and their research with the Gallup Poll Consulting Firm, identify some basic attributes: (1) maximize productivity focusing on strengths and managing weakness; (2) understanding strengths leads to identifying the difference between good and great outcomes; (3) leaders can make more effective decisions by focusing on what is right, versus what is wrong; and (4) optimal strengths develop when sufficient time management is focused on the subject matter or significant goal.

Positive police leaders self-monitor behaviors that derail progress. Self-control and the ability to delay gratification so that the greater good or excellence can be accomplished demand patience. The positive police leader's self-control, and the ability to restrain impulsive behaviors, represents important star performance personal qualities.

Becoming a positive police leader necessitates using emotional intelligence. This requires the ability to monitor one's emotional self-control, the basic requirement for leading police officers.

Daniel Goleman's book on *Emotional Intelligence* suggests that a leader's emotional intelligence quotient (EQ) is more important than the Intelligence Quotient (IQ). Self-management is the key to relationship management.

PROBLEM-SOLVING CORNER: LEADERSHIP INVENTORY

This Leadership Self-Rating Inventory represents an author-created, leadership self-assessment questionnaire. The inventory is not a validated scientific instrument. The goal: to explore areas that may offer opportunities for improvement and future leadership skill development. Readers who do not hold leadership positions may visualize how they may apply the leadership strategies. Refer to Table 12-1 for an illustration of a Leadership Self-Rating Inventory.

Table 12-1. Leadership Self-Rating Inventory

Personal Traits	1	2	3	4	5	6	7	8	9	10
Reads Others' Feelings										
Inspires Others										
Self-Awareness										
Social-Awareness										
Self-Management										
Relationship-Management										
Motivates Others										
Positive Teamwork										
Anger Management Skills										
Avoids Negative Behaviors										

The purpose of the inventory is to allow the reader to rate themselves using a 10-point general scale. Scores that range below 70% require additional study and training, 70–79% = average, 80–89% = above average, and 90–100% = Positive Leader Skills. Enjoy the self-exploration process. Only you, the reader, know the results of your self-assessment. Refer to Chapters 1–10 (Leadership Rating Inventories) that appear after the Epilogue Conclusion for additional self-assessment opportunities.

CONCLUSION

Sir Winston Churchill once noted: *"We make a living by what we get; we make a life by what we give."* Positive police leaders are givers, and police officers will follow their professional light. The following fundamental police paradigms highlight solutions that support positive and star performer leadership:

The "ILP Grand Theory" or policing paradigms: Intelligence-Led Policing (ILP) + Community-Oriented Policing (COP) + Problem-Oriented Policing (POP) + Neighborhood-Oriented Policing (NOP) + CompStat Tactical Operations (CTO) = Police Excellence (PE). This equation is the foundation for successful policing; ultimately, effective solutions augment the human side of policing. Therefore, the following equation is also necessary:

Community-Oriented Policing (COP) + Problem-Oriented Policing (POP) + Positive Leadership (PL) + Emotional Intelligence (EI) = Effective Policing Solutions (EPS).

Follow this pathway to successful interpersonal relationships that offer the gifts of inspirational leadership. Then problem-solving solutions will emerge in full view for decisive action. Positive police leaders take initiative and seize the moment.

LEADERSHIP SELF-RATING INVENTORIES

CHAPTER 1: Positive Police Pathways and Strategies

Table 1-1. Leadership Self-Rating Inventory

Personal Traits	1	2	3	4	5	6	7	8	9	10
Star Police Performer Abilities										
Emotional Intelligence Abilities										
Positive Leadership Abilities										
Intelligence-Led Policing Skills										
Community-Oriented Policing Skills										
Problem-Oriented Policing Skills										
Neighborhood-Oriented Policing Skills										
SARA Planning Skills										
CompStat Operations Skills										
Paradigm Synchronization Skills										

CHAPTER 2: Positive Police Strategic Leadership Strategies

Table 2-1. Leadership Self-Rating Inventory

Personal Traits	1	2	3	4	5	6	7	8	9	10
Strategic Vision Abilities										
Leadership Clarity Abilities										
Telling the Strategic Story										
Intelligence Cycle Abilities										
Partnering Relationships										
Rewriting the Mission Abilities										
Addressing the Comfort Zone										
Reorganization of Structure										
Tactical Applications										
Developing Specialized Teams										

CHAPTER 3: Positive Police Leadership: Finding the Pathway

Table 3-1. Leadership Self-Rating Inventory

Personal Traits	1	2	3	4	5	6	7	8	9	10
Special Calling Identification										
Professional Integrity										
Professional Ethics										
Golden Rule Applications										
Loyalty to Others										
Honesty in Relationships										
Candor in Relationships										
Truthfulness										
Participatory Management										
Delegation of Authority										

CHAPTER 4: Positive Motivational Leadership: Finding the Way

Table 4-1. Leadership Self-Rating Inventory

Personal Traits	1	2	3	4	5	6	7	8	9	10
Professional Role Model										
Inspirational Leadership										
Self- Motivation										
Motivation of Officers										
Officer Goal Achievement										
Responsibility for Officers' Welfare										
Motivation: Officer Achievement										
Creative Solutions										
Maslow's Self-Fulfillment										
Maslow's Transcendence										

CHAPTER 5: Positive Problem-Solving Communication

Table 5-1. Leadership Self-Rating Inventory

Personal Traits	1	2	3	4	5	6	7	8	9	10
Applies Strategic Communication Skills										
Applies Elements of Communication										
Applies Communication Clarity										
Applies Active Listening										
Applies the Strategic Message										
Use of the Channels of Communication										
Conducts Effective Staff Briefings										
Leadership Communication Credibility										
Execution of the Effective Message										
Applies Information Sharing										

CHAPTER 6: Positive Problem-Solving Training

Table 6-1. Leadership Self-Rating Inventory

Personal Traits	1	2	3	4	5	6	7	8	9	10
Addresses POP Training Needs										
Focuses on Field Training										
Values Spontaneous Field Training										
Develops Diverse Training Cycles										
Developing Critical Incident Training										
Provides Team Training										
Defines the Training Philosophy										
Develops Training Goals										
Develops Training Objectives										
Conducts Training Evaluation										

CHAPTER 7: Positive Strategic Planning, Evaluation and Assessment

Table 7-1. Leadership Self-Rating Inventory

Personal Traits	1	2	3	4	5	6	7	8	9	10
Promotes Positive POP Changes										
Vision Focus Traits										
Strategic Planning Skills										
Implementing Vision										
Mission Statement Focus										
Demonstrates Values Statement										
Addresses Strengths										
Addresses Weaknesses										
Addresses Goals										
Provides Leadership Direction										

CHAPTER 8: Positive SARA Planning

Table 8-1. Leadership Self-Rating Inventory

Personal Traits	1	2	3	4	5	6	7	8	9	10
Thinks Outside the Box										
Implements SARA Planning										
Staff Study Skills										
Scope of the Problem Skills										
Statement of the Problem Skills										
POP Narrative Description Skills										
Applies SMART Skills										
POP Project Action Plan Skills										
POP Project Work Plan Skills										
POP Appraisal Skills										

CHAPTER 9: Positive Problem-Solving: POP Projects

Table 9-1. Leadership Self-Rating Inventory

Personal Traits	1	2	3	4	5	6	7	8	9	10
POP Problem Response Skills										
POP Project Development Skills										
Positive Assumption Recognition Skills										
Negative Assumption Recognition Skills										
Crime Analysis Skills										
POP Stage Assessment Skills										
Risk Management Skills										
Decision Paper Writing Skills										
Deployment Strategy Skills										
CompStat Tactical Skills										

CHAPTER 10: Positive Coaching: Police Operations

Table 10-1. Leadership Self-Rating Inventory

Personal Traits	1	2	3	4	5	6	7	8	9	10
Basic Coaching Skills										
Applies the Elements of Coaching										
Active Listening Skills										
Enhances Officer Potential Skills										
Asks Questions Skills										
Establishing Rapport Skills										
Mutual Understanding Skills										
Identifies Unproductive Behaviors										
Rewards the Correct Behaviors										
Problem-Solving Flexibility Skills										

BIBLIOGRAPHY AND FURTHER READINGS

Baker, Thomas, *Effective Police Leadership: Moving Beyond Management* (New York, New York: Looseleaf Law Publications, Inc., 3rd Edition, 2011).

Baker, Thomas, *Intelligence-Led Policing: Leadership, Strategies and Tactics* (New York, New York: Looseleaf Law Publications, Inc., 2009).

Baker, Thomas and Loreen Wolfer, "The Crime Triangle: Alcohol, Drug Use and Vandalism," *International Journal of Police Practice and Research*, 4, (2003): 47–61.

Bartlett, David, *Making your Point: Communicating Effectively with Audiences of One to One Million* (New York, New York: St. Martin's Press, 2008).

Bennis, Warren, *Why Leaders Can't Lead* (San Francisco, California: Jossey-Bass Publishers, 1989).

Bennis, Warren, "The Challenges of Leadership in the Modern World," *American Psychologist* (62, no. 1 2007): 2–5.

Blake, Robert and Jane S. Mouton, "A 9.9 Approach to Increasing Organizational Productivity." In E. H. Schein and W. G. Bennis (Eds.) *Personal Organizational and Change Through Group Methods* (New York, Wiley, 1965): 169–183.

Bradbury, Travis and Jean Greaves, Emotional Intelligence, 2.0 (San Diego: California: TalentSmart, 2009).

Bynum, Timothy, *Using Analysis for Problem-Solving: A Guidebook for Law Enforcement,* U.S. Department of Justice: Community Oriented Policing Services (Washington DC: GPO, 2002).

Bynum, Timothy, *Using Analysis for Problem-Solving: A Guidebook for Law Enforcement,* U.S. Department of Justice, Office of Community-Oriented Policing (Washington, DC: GPO September, 2001).

Clarke, Ronald V. and John E. Eck, *Crime Analysis for Problem-Solvers: In 60 Small Steps*, U.S. Department of Justice: Community Oriented Policing Services (Washington DC: GPO, 2005).

Cherniss, Cary and Daniel Goleman, *The Emotionally Intelligent Workplace: How to Select for, Measure, and Improve Emotional Intelligence in Individuals, Groups and Organizations* (San Francisco, California: Jossey-Bass, 2001).

Covey, Stephen, *The Seven Habits of Highly Effective People* (New York: Simon and Schuster, 1990).

Covey, Stephen, *The 8th Habit: From Effectiveness to Greatness* (New York, New York: Free Press, 2004), 5.

Clifton, Donald and Paula Nelson, *Soar with Your Strengths* (New York: Delacorte Press, 1992).

Eck, John, *Assessing Responses to Problems: An Introductory Guide for Police Problem-Solvers*, U.S. Department of Justice: Community Oriented Policing Services (Washington DC: GPO, 2002).

"Facilitators' Guide to the RCMP Learning Maps: CAPRA Problem Solving Model" (Ottawa, Ontario: *Royal Canadian Mounted Police, 1993*).

Fuentes, Joseph R. et al., New Jersey State Police: Practical Guide to Intelligence-Led Policing, the Center of Policing Terrorism at the Manhattan Institute, September 2006, 3.

Fournies, Ferniand, *Coaching for Improved Performance* (New York, New York: McGraw-Hill, 2000).

Global Intelligence Working Group, "National Criminal Intelligence Sharing Plan," October 2003, 2.

Giuliani, Rudolph W. and Howard Safir, *COMPSTAT: Leadership in Action* (New York: New York City Police Department, 1997), 2–7.

Goleman, Daniel, *Emotional Intelligence: Why It Matters More Than IQ* (New York, New York: Bantam Books, 1995), 34.

Goleman, Daniel, *Working with Emotional Intelligence* (New York: Bantam Books, 1998).

Goldstein, Herman, *Problem Oriented Policing: A Practical Guide for Police Officers* (New York: McGraw-Hill Publishing Company, 1990).

Henry, Vincent, *The CompStat Paradigm: Management Accountability in Policing, Business and the Public Sector* (New York: Looseleaf Law Publications, Inc., 2003).

Hertzberg, Fredrick, and B. B. Snyderman, *Motivation to Work* (New York, Wiley, 1959).

International Association of Law Enforcement Intelligence Analysts (IALEIA), "Law Enforcement Analytical Standards," November 2004: 3.

Jeary, Tony, *Strategic Acceleration: Success at the Speed of Life* (New York, NY: Vanguard Press, 2009).

Kelley, Robert, *How to be a Star at Work* (New York: Times Books, 1998).

Maslow, Abraham, *Motivation and Personality, 2 Ed.* (New York: Harper and Row, 1970).

Nadler, Reldan, *Leading with Emotional Intelligence* (New York, NY: McGraw-Hill, companies, Inc., 2011).

National Criminal Intelligence Service, United Kingdom, "The National Intelligence Model" (London, England, 2000): 8.

Peterson, Christopher, *Primer in Positive Psychology* (New York, New York: Oxford University Press, 2006).

Peterson, Marilyn, *Intelligence-Led Policing: The New Intelligence Architecture*, U.S. Department of Justice, Bureau of Justice Assistance (Washington, DC: GPO, 2005).

Rath, Tom and Barry Conchie, *Strengths Based Leadership: Great Leaders, Teams and Why People Follow* (New York, NY: Gallup Press, Inc., 2008).

Richards, Dick, *Convincing Minds and Moving Hearts* (Louisville, KY: Brown Herron Punishing, 2002).

Ryan, Richard and Edward Deci, "Self-Determination Theory and the Facilitation of Intrinsic Motivation, Social Development, and Well-Being," *The American Psychologist*, (55(1), 2000): 68–78.

Seligman, Martin, *Authentic Happiness: Using the New Positive Psychology to Realize Your Potential* (New York, New York: Knopf, 2002).

Scott, Michael and Herman Goldstein, *Shifting and Sharing Responsibility for Public Safety Problems*, U.S. Department of Justice: Community Oriented Policing Services (Washington DC: GPO, 2005).

Thibault, Edward A., Lawrence M. Lynch, and R. Bruce McBride, *Proactive Leadership* (Upper Saddle River: New Jersey, 2001).

Thurman, Quint C. and J. D. Jamieson, Eds., *Police Problem-Solving* (Cincinnati, Ohio: Anderson Press Publishing, 2004).

United States Army Field Manual 101-5, Staff Organization and Operations, May 31, 1997.

United Kingdom Home Office, "Operational Policing: National Intelligence Model," Internet URL, London England, 2006.

U.S. Department of Justice, Bureau of Justice Assistance, Understanding Community Policing (Washington DC: GPO, 1995).

U.S. Department of Justice, Bureau of Justice Assistance, Neighborhood-Oriented Policing in Rural Communities: A Program Planning Guide (Washington, DC: GPO, 1994).

Vroom, Victor H. *Work and Motivation* (New York: Wiley, 1964); Victor H. Vroom, "Leadership and Decision-Making," *Organizational Dynamics* (Spring 2000): 82-94.

Whisenand, Paul M. and R. Fred Ferguson, *The Managing of Police Organizations* (New Jersey: Simon & Schuster Co., 2001).

Zenger, John and Folkman, Joseph, *The Extraordinary Leader* (New York: McGraw-Hill, 2002).

INDEX